Growing Up Gateway

By Mike Westveer

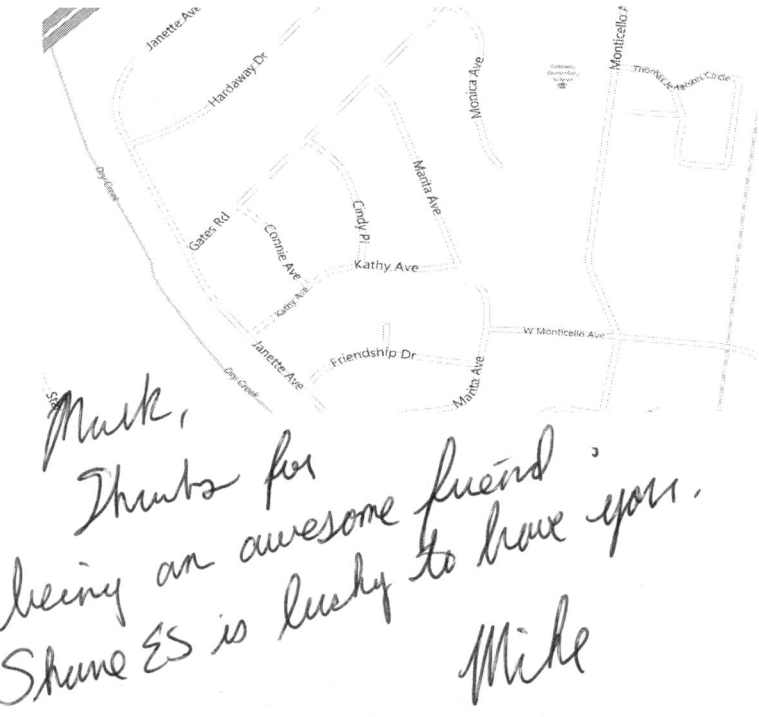

Mark,
Thanks for being an awesome friend. Shane ES is lucky to have you.

Mike

This book is dedicated to my wife Dana and our three children Dallas, Brady, and Presley.

Also, to the Gateway Gang. Thanks for the friendships; both then and now.

Contents

The Creek

School

Sports

Bikes

Fun Times

Holidays

Church

Friends of the Family

Fishing

Relatives

In Closing

Chapter 1
The Creek

Near the southern end of Gateway subdivision in Goodlettsville, Tennessee, behind the houses that lined Janette Avenue, ran the world's most unbelievable playground, where countless hours were spent, and an untold number of memories made. Officially named Dry Creek, but lovingly called "the Creek", I spent many of my childhood days enjoying the treasures that the creek held for me, my brother, and our friends.

Dry Creek was very seldom that, dry. Though it did occasionally run below its normal stage, most of the time it was flowing strong, and in and around its waters lived a wonderland of adventures for school aged boys looking for fun and a break from the normal routine. Never did a day repeat itself at the creek. Each day was unique in the way it unfolded. Even when we had every minute planned, the creek often chose to make its own plans.

I don't recall exactly when I was introduced to the creek, but it was in the early elementary grades. The creek was a destination where I longed to be if I wasn't actually there. The creek was open from dusk to dawn and our main entrance was at the bottom of Friendship Drive. My family lived at the top of the hill in the middle of Friendship Court. A downhill hike to Janette Avenue via Friendship Drive, through the center of two middle class brick homes, placed us in our natural paradise. We could jump on our bikes and coast the entire way to begin each adventure if we chose to do so.

    Seldom did I venture to the creek alone. This wasn't due to fear or any other reason than it was more fun playing and exploring with friends. The usual gang included my brother Ray and our neighbors, the Lewis boys; David, Ryan, and Tim. Occasionally someone outside that inner circle would join the fun. It was fun showing a rookie the ropes, but not near the fun as spending time with the veterans. Regardless of the crew that was a part of that day's journey, we were in for a treat.

    When we set out on our trek to the creek, there was no mystery in where we were headed. In our tow would be a variety of items depending on the mission of the day. Supplies might include buckets, fishing poles, nets, tackle boxes, snacks, and bait. Sometimes our bait became a snack and on very special days when the fish outlasted our bait, our snack became bait. Mom knew to buy extra bologna or sliced cheese to feed our habit.

    Occasionally we would ride to the creek on our bikes. Have you ever tried to balance buckets, fishing poles, and friends on a bike going downhill ninety to nothing? To step up the difficulty, sometimes the buckets would be full of water and the previous day's catch to be released back into the creek. That balancing act was a sight to be seen. Showing off this talent for our neighbors the Campbell girls, or any other unsuspecting onlooker was done with great pride.

    The chosen point of entry into the creek was also where we spent most of our time. We didn't have an actual name for this part of the creek, but that didn't stop us from creating non-stop fun. I'm not sure if the property owners at this part of the creek worked all the time or just didn't care that we used their yard as a launching point, but they never voiced objections to our presence or the pile of bikes that were left unattended in their yard. My best guess is they longed to be in the middle of the fun with us.

    Minnows were the major draw at this portion of the creek. Not since Gilligan has there been so much fun had with a minnow. This part of the creek was loaded with these tiny fish. Sometimes the bottom looked like one huge glimmering mass. On the rare occasion that we stood still, usually from exhaustion, the movements of the schooling minnows became mesmerizing. The ninety-nine percent of the time we were going full tilt, the goal was to try to catch as many of these creatures as possible.

    We even named the different types of minnows found in the creek. Some were named for obvious physical features such as the Top Water. These minnows were massive (as far as minnows go), pushing three inches in length with a very distinctive white spot right in the middle of their back. They were light silver in color, very sleek looking, and the fastest moving animal in the water, including us. If they had possessed a dorsal fin that rose up out of the water, it would have appeared that miniature Great Whites stalked the lesser minnows. They were truly a trophy catch.

Top Waters seldom schooled in large groups. In fact, if two were seen in close proximity, we had struck gold. Most of the time these giants were loners, and very elusive, the gold medal of minnowing. The sheer thrill of landing a "big one" caused us to be imaginative in our fishing.

Like almost everything we do in life, catching Top Waters took practice and lots of trial and error, not to mention lots of innovation, too. As rookies in the early years, we splashed many a mile aimlessly chasing these guys, only to end up empty handed. We didn't even come close enough to a catch to make up a fisherman's tale.

While there was plenty of fun to be had in the chase, the satisfaction of a catch eluded us in the beginning. Our one hundred percent group effort was no match for the Top Water in his own environment.

The creek environment was an amazing one. The water in this stretch of creek was approximately nine inches deep during normal conditions and flowed at a steady pace. The upstream section was fairly rock free and slightly shallower. The creek bottom was very interesting and unique in this section. It consisted of thousands of divots, giving the impression that some of the occupants of the creek were constantly working with their pitching wedges. The water's erosion power was a fascinating artist. The downstream portion was slightly deeper, with a pocket of deeper water on the far side of the creek. That pocket is where the majority of the creek's wildlife chose to congregate the majority of the time.

    Not only was the creek bed bumpy, it was slick. A thin layer of creek muck covered every inch of the floor. We chose to ignore what this material must have consisted of and how it came to be. Taking a step in this muck was in and of itself an adventure. An ice rink has nothing on this type of creek bottom. To say it was slick would be like saying the ocean has water in it. It was hard to keep your footing and the creek seemed to take pleasure in sending us for a spill. Getting wet from head to toe wasn't necessarily a bad thing, especially in the heat of the summer, but the fall often came with a knot, scrap, or bruise. Again, this wasn't necessarily a bad thing. A visible battle wound can bring many accolades from friends and classmates, your choice of character band-aids, and some relished pamper time with Mom (of course, not to be done in sight of friends).

Determined not to be outdone by Mr. Minnow, we had to come up with plan B. Plan A was unstructured chaos and was a total failure. We simply weren't going to be able to chase down those guys. How could we get these fish from the creek and into our possession? Our next strategy was to narrow the playing field, trying to turn the advantage in our favor. We decided there was just too much space for the minnow to maneuver.

Attempt number one in our newly developed plan B was to use what was readily available and in abundance, rocks. While upstream was rock free, downstream was rock city. These rocks came in all shapes and sizes and did not resist being brought into service. Through trail and error we started placing and stacking rocks to form makeshift dams, funneling the minnows where we wished.

Watch out Top Water, your reign was soon to be over. Narrower space, splash, splash, splash, wet clothes, new bruises, zero minnows. Bummer! Now it was time for Plan B, part 2. Having all been successful members of athletic teams, we decided that we needed to try using teamwork. The playing field was already established and now Team Creek was ready to rumble.

Depending on the numbers of creekers in the line-up that day, a portion of us would stand downstream and prepare to nab our catch for the day. The remainder of the group would head upstream.

The Top Water Round-Up was about to begin in Gateway's Dry Creek. Those of us upstream would start the rush downstream. This was a sight to behold in and of itself. You'd have thought we were running for our lives, being chased by some horrifying predator. We high-stepped down the creek, splashing water in every direction, all the while yelling out instructions to each other. Most of the splashing occurred from the high-stepping, but some occurred from one or more of us losing our balance and slipping on the muck covered bottom. Watch out if the person in front of the charge went down. It inevitably led to a chain reaction pile up with the entire crew drenched. Much like cars pilling up on an ice covered street, the slick creek bed did not allow for sudden stops.

If even one teammate went down, the attempt was bungled. The first person to realize the failure was the one who caused the breach. It was instantly known by the Top Waters that there was now a way out, and the minnows went for the opening.

The reason the downed kid was the first to know had nothing to do with sight, but everything to do with touch. Personal space is not important to these minnows when a huge figure has splashed down into their world. What was important was to get away, and do so immediately.

Part of what happens during this attack is the

muddying of the waters, literally and figuratively. Literally, mud and muck get pushed from the bottom and into the current, giving the big, bad Top Water minnow cover to make his escape. Figuratively, order is propelled into chaos.

Even the lonely Top Water has structure to its swimming. Straight paths, with an occasional change in direction when coming into contact with an obstacle or another creature, are the normal activity of this giant. When we inserted ourselves into the equation, any appearance of routine vanished.

The outcome of this created chaos was the fallen boy being pelted by super-hyper Top Waters trying frantically to escape. While I wouldn't describe this feeling as physically excruciating, it is definitely painful emotionally to have your prey "poking" fun at you and then going cheerfully on his way. Again, big-time bummer!

Not knowing the meaning of give up, we brainstormed what our next step should be. We were in a great place to have been a total failure and still having the time of our lives.

One thing that became evident was that to trap our target, we had to be upright on our feet, not lying horizontal in the creek being pummeled by our adversary. The decision became to herd the slippery Top Water minnow at a slow, steady pace. We hoped this method would end the splash-downs that gave the minnow an escape route. Walking was still very unsteady on this surface, but it was much easier than doing the high-step boogie at full velocity.

So back to our starting points we went and once again set our sights on our elusive target. With our downstream catcher in position, we set off with a deliberate pace, sweeping back and forth to force the minnows towards their capture. It was tough to control the excitement and not just surge forward, but we knew from previous experiences that an all out rush just wasn't going to work.

The trapper would stand near the previously built dam, feet angled in a Vee shape to help funnel in the fish, back arched over, hands out away from the body, ready to snatch out any Mr. Minnow that dared stray too close. This new method proved to have potential. The targets were heading towards our trap. Would this be our first taste of success?

When the Top Waters were in between the catcher's shoes or feet, the moment of truth was at hand. A quick, two-handed scoop all the way to the bottom of the creek was a must. In the midst of the stirred up muck and captured rocks hopefully awaited a minnow. If you've managed to land the Top Water, you instantly knew.

The Top Water is a strong species and doesn't appreciate confinement, much less the inability to breathe. So trapping the minnow was just the start, getting to show him off to your buddies was the icing on the cake.

GOTCHA!!! Quickly to the bank we headed

to gloat, brag, and marvel at the trophy, hoping a quick wiggle didn't send the big fellow back into the drink. Once ashore with the safety net of land under us, we quickly become both scientists and statisticians.

"That's the biggest one I've ever caught", "He'll turn into a bass when he's bigger", "If he stays out of the water too long the others won't swim with him anymore", and numerous other improvable statements and bragging would be shared.

After the initial enthusiasm waned we began to ponder our next move. Usually the answer was quick and easy, let him go and let's catch a "bigger, better, and badder" one. The catcher definitely got the honor of releasing the minnow back into the creek so he could grow into that mammoth largemouth. This too involved into a game. Who could track the released minnow the longest? In the case of 'o Toppy, no one ever succeeded for very long.

We got really efficient at minnow wrangling and soon looked to take it to the next level, buckets. Five gallon buckets with a wire handle quickly became a necessity at Dry Creek. What hands could previously do, now buckets would do with greater success and ease, increasing our daily catch rate immensely.

These buckets were placed at the strategic opening surrounded by the previously built rock dam. We submerged the buckets in the creek and tried to disguise their appearance by carefully placing rocks and muck around its opening.

An advantage to this newest approach was that it freed another person to join in the herding of the minnows. The first person reaching the bucket would simply turn it on end, careful not to tip its contents over. Next was the excitement of seeing what, if anything, our catch would turn out to include. The creek was flourishing with so much life; rarely did we come up with a totally empty bucket.

Having the bucket brought a brand new thought to our minds. Now we could actually transport our haul somewhere if we wished. Joining the tradition that fishermen have long promoted, we wanted to show off old Toppy to those who remained ashore.

Mom and Dad knew of our adventures to the creek and usually approved, or at least, consented to our going. They graciously listened to our tales of adventures and put up with our creek soiled clothing and damp, smelly shoes lined up outside the den against the chimney. Getting to show them our daily catch was very exciting.

We quickly found out that minnows couldn't survive long in a bucket, so we had to come up with another way of keeping them alive. Minnows were used to flowing water, full of oxygen. A bucket of stagnant water quickly became unlivable. Off and on in my childhood I had assorted fish tanks and goldfish bowls, coming and going with the whims of an active child. An obvious answer to where to house the minnows was in these dusty, unused tanks. However, after a few seconds it became obvious this answer was not feasible. Berserk would be a tempered way of putting into words what happened in the first moments after transferring the Top Water from the bucket into the tank or fishbowl.

A fish who is used to having a creek as home doesn't appreciate anything hindering his movement, regardless of the shape or size. More water ended up on the floor than in the bowl. Apparently fish can't knock themselves out, because if they could, we would have witnessed fish la-la land. And if there happened to be a tank mate, the old saying of being in the wrong place at the wrong time came to the forefront. There would not be creek minnows living in my aquarium.

One of the crazier things we attempted was a minnow farm. The Lewis backyard was the choice for this attempt at connecting home and creek. We turned our Wiffle Ball Wrigley into a series of hand dug canals. Years of daily ballgames had worn many grassless patches in the yard which was to become our version of Dry Creek North. Just add water and, wahlah, we had ourselves a minnow farm.

The water came from the faucet on the backside of the Lewis house. The now very valuable buckets were put to use to haul the water from the sprig to the newly dug canals. We filled up each portion of our farm and introduced the minnows to their new home.

As kids seem to do, we quickly changed our focus to something else. Video games, television, bike riding, or a challenge from a neighborhood team was probably what drew our attention away from our new construction. Returning later in the day, dreams clashed with reality.

The minnows were still there but the water wasn't. David would work in the field of aquatic structures later in life but this attempt would not be worthy of placing on his resume'. We imagined the ditches to be like bowls. Pour the water in and it would stay there. We learned the hard way that the real world was quite different. Freshly manipulated soil makes a great absorber and the water quickly seeped into the dirt. The minnows paid the ultimate price for a group of boys' whims. Our defunct minnow farm should have also bore the name Dry Creek.

The last attempt to provide Mr. Top Water with a home away from home would be to just house the minnows in the bucket. We had an out building that sat in our backyard, next to our paved driveway/basketball court. Between the side of the building and the fence separating our yard from the Pruitt's yard was a three foot walkway where we stored our trash cans. Due to a scraggily old tree and seasonal blossoming honeysuckle, this area remained shady for the greater part of the day. This appeared to be the perfect spot for raising bucketbound minnows.

After returning from the creek with another haul, we were determined that this would be the answer. We placed the bucket in the shade between the out building and the honeysuckle filled fence. We would change the water often, thus providing the minnows with plenty of oxygen. Just as before, interest waned and our bikes took us elsewhere.

Upon returning later in the day, we were fired up to see our Creekians still kicking. We were instantly experts in the field of minnowing. We brought home live fish, and hours later they were still swimming. High five, baby! We can breed them, sell them, keep them for pets; this opened up numerous options for us, or so we thought.

In actuality, watching our catch swim around in circles in a bucket quickly became boring. Another thing that tamed our interest was the disgusting odor of those that didn't make it back to the creek. Though it was really neat having success in keeping live minnows at home, the newness wore off and the thrill faded. Minnows were best left at the creek, much to the relief of the many strong-nosed dogs having to smell our failures.

The Top Water was the beast of the creek, but by far not the only fish in the water. Jumping on the bandwagon of the newly established baseball card companies of the early eighties, we nicknamed the Top Water "Topps" after the long standing company, and named two other varieties Fleer and Donruss, after the fledgling up and comers. Another version was the Stripper, a medium size fellow with a bass like dark stripe down its side, thus his name.

Possibly the oddest looking minnow was the bottom dwellers we called suckers. These creatures skimmed the bottom looking for their next meal and were not very populous. They had flat bottom sides and were thicker than the average minnow. They possessed a black and brown marble patterned skin that was really fascinating. Catching these guys was very rare and very exciting, more luck than skill.

Minnow encounters were a blast and never failed to provide a day of entertainment, but they were far from the only source of entertainment at the creek. At the same section of creek, just a few feet downstream, was the source of another chance for excitement. This is where the creek's flow slowed just a bit and leveled off in depth. It was approximately five inches deep and rock strewn. The current of the creek had established the route that the water would take trough the rocks. It created an illusion of there being several creeks in one with the water splitting here and there before rejoining itself downstream.

The rocks ranged from tiny stones to almost immovable ones. Some were smoothed by the steady running water while others remained very rough. Some rocks were totally immersed in the water while others sat almost completely dry above the creek, perched upon other rocks.

We considered these rocks pieces of a puzzle

for us to manipulate as we saw fit. If we wanted to cross the creek without getting wet, we would move the rocks to form stepping stones. In the case of minnowing, we would move the rocks into position to help us trap our prey. And of course, most boys just enjoy throwing rocks and skipping them across the water.

Something started to occur when we began moving rocks. We noticed many strange creatures were in fact living under the rocks. One of the strangest things was the crawdad. A crawdad, sometimes called a crawfish in other parts of the country, looks like a miniature lobster. They range from tiny specimen no more than one-half inch long to menacing monsters, a good six inches in length with claws capable of doing some damage.

Most of the crawdads were brownish gray in color. Some sported tinges of red, yellow, or black. They had large heads with minuscule, beady eyes on each side. Extending from the head were two antennas. The backs of the crawdads consisted of a very hard shell, with bendable sections. Below the back was the tail, their source of quick movement. It was shaped like a fan with very little points jutting out, much like a broom. The crawdads had six legs, each looking like a tiny twig. The underside of each crawdad was lighter than the backs, usually a pale brown color.

Unlike the minnow, there was a bit of "danger" in the hunt for the crawdad. These guys came equipped with two pinchers and could deliver quite the wallop. Extending from the middle of the body were two "arms" that had the crawdads natural protection and food gathering devices on the ends. These claws would not close completely from top to bottom. They were crescent shaped which allowed the ends to meet, but the middle would not quite close the gap. On the inside parts of each claw were ridges, not sharp, but very rough. I assume these were used for the crawdad to keep in place whatever it had captured.

At first, most of us were very curious, yes, but also a bit fearful. Now, you would never hear any of us admit to being afraid, but it was true. The one exception may have been Ryan. This middle Lewis boy could have cared less about the pinchers and was known the pick up anything that moved without regard for safety or the consequences. We couldn't decide if he was really brave or just stupid. I think probably a little of both.

Was it possible that we could capture these guys like we had the minnows? More importantly, could it be done without permanent injury? The curiosity of the crawdad was more than the minds of young boys could, or would, ignore. The task became, much like that of the minnows, to find out how to bring about their capture.

Crawdads were unlike minnows in most every way. Yes, they shared Dry Creek as a home, but that is where the similarities stopped. Minnows love to dart about, exploring the creek and its inhabitants. Crawdads usually remained stationary, preferring to hide under a rock, unseen. Most minnows schooled while crawdads were loners. Minnows became helpless out of water, crawdads continue to put up a good fight. Probably the oddest difference was in movement. Minnows swam forward, occasionally darting from side to side to change direction. Crawdads moved backwards, using a large, strong tail to propel themselves through the rocks and water. Knowing the way they moved became a huge asset in our hunt.

The previously used and perfected herding techniques would definitely not work with the crawdad. This hunt would be a much slower paced activity as well as an individual one. However, the excitement of what we would find would be just as intense.

Crawdads, for the most part, stayed hidden under rocks. So to find the creatures, we would turn over rocks, wait for the current to carry the muck away, and see if a crawdad had chosen that rock for a home. Choosing the right rock to turn over was a skill within itself. We figured out what size and what placement of the rock would give us the best chance to find a crawdad.

The rock needed to be totally, or at least mostly, underwater. The preferred size was about six inches across and flat. Also, the rock should be out of any strong current. The removal of the rock was extremely important. We learned to lift the rock from the most upstream part, raising it until it stood straight up. Then the rock must be lifted straight up out of the water. This allowed for the least disturbance to the crawdads and their surroundings. If you were good at this technique, the disturbance of the muck was minimal and the crawdad wasn't crushed by the moving rock.

Hopefully after the water cleared, we would see a crawdad sitting in the crater left behind. Now the hard part began. Ever so slowly, we placed our hands above the water, directly atop the exposed crawdad. Our hands would be held in a pinching position, with fingers and thumb spread apart. While making as little disturbance as possible, we would push our hand into the water towards the target. When our hand reached approximately an inch above the crawdad, it was time to act. Pushing down as quickly as possible, we reached the critter. The target area was the hard shell just below the head, with thumb on one side and fingers on the other.

Usually the capture included pinning the crawdad to the bottom of the creek while we manipulated our hands into the best possible position. If we were able to reach that position, the crawdad was ours. By grabbing in this particular area, we not only got a secure hold of the crawdad, but were also protecting ourselves from a pinch.

The victory pose was struck if we were

successful. The arm would burst out of the water, flinging water everywhere, and raised high above the head with crawdad on display. "Got one" or "Oh, yeah" would be the often heard statement at the creek bed. If the catch was extraordinary, everyone would gather around to see the giant. The biggest crawdad I remember seeing was about seven inches in length. The big guy only had one claw. We made up stories about what great creature had gotten the best of this fellow. However, the remaining claw was more than ready to inflict pain to anyone or thing that dared cross its path.

 When we hunted crawdads, the bucket was always with us. Little did we know there was some great entertainment taking place inside that bucket. As we hunted, we would toss each catch into the bucket and continue looking for our next victim. Not until later did we notice the titanic clashes occurring in the bucket. These loners didn't appreciate visitors, nor did they appreciate being out in the open without cover.

 These combatants were at war with one another. Pinchers were cocked and ready to attack. Larger crawdads had literally pinched and picked up some of the smaller ones, holding them high in the air. Equally sized guys had hold of one another. A creek side battle royal had commenced. You think that wasn't something worth watching as a young boy? We named the crawdads after the famous wrestlers of the day, Jerry "The King" Lawler, Tojo Yamamoto,

Dutch Mantell, Andre the Giant, and others.

The next step was to set up matches between chosen combatants. We would empty the bucket except for the two participants and let them go at it. Yes, as I look back, it seems sort of cruel, but as a young boy, it was too great to pass up. We began searching the rocks for the next great crawdad champion.

One thing that we did take part in that we all knew crossed the line into cruelty was to place minnows and crawdads in the bucket at the same time. Those minnows didn't have a prayer and would soon end up as shish kebabs in the pinchers of the crawdads. In their tiny brains, the crawdads surely appreciated such an easily caught meal.

The activity of turning over rocks brings me to another part of creek lore. Crawdads are not the only animal that enjoy the comfort of a cold, dark, damp rock. Though we did not come across lots of snakes, they were a part of Dry Creek. Although rocks were their choice of cover also, it was rocks that were away from the water or in very shallow, still water that they favored. As long as we were in the creek, removing rocks from the current, we weren't afraid of running into a snake.

However, the Dry Creek Dundee, Ryan Lewis, would occasionally set out to find a snake. Being too tough to admit to being scared, the others and I would take part also. I was smart enough to choose rocks very unlikely to house a snake while still appearing brave enough to hunt. However, if I happened to flip a rock over and find a snake, I pressed on to save face.

The first step was to alert the others to a snake so we could surround the serpent. The next step was to capture the creature. Now, depending on who was doing the capturing, various and extreme techniques were used.

Ryan would just scoop up the creature with his hand, throwing caution to the wind. Of course, this would result in him being bitten occasionally, but apparently it didn't hurt enough to cause him to choose a safer method. Ryan knew lots about animals, especially snakes. He knew the different kinds of snakes and was very aware that the snakes we uncovered were non-poisonous and probably more scared of us than we were of them. The most frequent find was a water snake, usually about six inches in length. It was black on the top side with a lighter, yellowish underbelly.

I don't recall trying to keep, breed, or sale any of the captured snakes. Ryan sometimes chose to take one home and keep it in one of his many aquariums, but most snakes were freed after a short examination.

We were very aware that snakes were in our midst as we romped around the creek and its surroundings. However, one snake encounter that will never escape my mind happened in close proximity to where we spent the majority of our time.

The gang had been "up the creek" doing some creek gallivanting and were on our way back to the usual stomping grounds. We were coming up on the crater part of minnow alley when out of the corner of my eye something caught my attention. Coiled up near the bank of the creek was the biggest snake I had ever laid eyes on. This monster was wrapped tightly around itself, basking in the sun, while enjoying about an inch of water on its underside. Wrapped up upon himself, he sat a good five inches high. Though we had been unaware of him, he knew exactly where we were and that we were too close to his space.

    I'm sure I must have peed all over myself, but already being wet from top to bottom, I'm unsure. Being too scared to scream, my flailing arms and back stroke motion quickly got the attention of the others. Now remember, this part of the creek was comparable to walking on ice. We could not have done more wrong in trying to escape being eaten whole.

    Not knowing then what I know now still scares me when I think about it. We should have quietly made our way away from the snake, creating the least disturbance as possible. Instead, we nearly created a tidal wave that must have seemed like a threat to the big guy. Luckily, the snake had just eaten, was too comfortable to move, or just didn't think we were worth the bother. What ever the case, he just watched us make a fool of ourselves and kept on basking. Thank you snake!

After we scurried out of harm's way and reached the bank, our curiosity kicked in. After recounting to each other how close to death we had actually been, catching our breath, saying a prayer of thanks (or a few Rosary's in the Lewis boy's case),and trying not to run home crying "Momma", we decided to get a second look.

The snake was located about a foot and a half below the bank. We figured if we were careful, we could get a look at the gigantic snake without putting ourselves in danger a second time that day. We did get to look at the big guy, but then a horrible thing happened. The snake slithered into a nearby hole and disappeared.

The reason this was such an ill-fated situation was that now we would never know when this fellow was lurking nearby. Our previously safe place now became a place of leeriness. Our next few trips to the creek were a little less enjoyable than before this encounter. Who knew when the coiled creature would make its next appearance? Our little minds created the most awful predictions. Maybe there was a mate, what if it was a den, what if the one we saw was just a baby, etc. Luckily, as time passed so did our fears. We never saw the snake again, but that one meeting was plenty for me and the rest of the gang.

Intermittently along the creek were very small water falls of about a foot in height. If you peered closely underneath the rock ledges, you could see several pairs of snake eyes staring back at you. This turned into an opportunity to have some great fun. We would spend hours at a time throwing rocks at the snakes. We did this at a safe distance, probably because of the earlier scare.

My brother Ray would later up the ante' by bringing his BB gun to the creek. Those little rascals provided great practice on improving our shooting skills. The only problem was patience. Every time you threw a rock or took a shot, the little guys would retreat into their holes only to return approximately a minute later.

As we widened our boundaries at the creek, we discovered a few places that looked worthy of fishing. The first was as far upstream as we ventured. Nicknamed "the bridge", such a fishing spot was a dream come true. This spot became our new favorite. It was at the curve of Janette Avenue before the street rose uphill towards Alta Loma Boulevard. Located behind some of the few two story houses in the Gateway subdivision was this jewel of a find. Just below the hustle and bustle of Interstate 65 was a fishing hole. To get to the spot you had to first cross the creek at a very narrow section. This led you to a landing, strewn with rocks dried by the sun, looking very similar to a rock laden beach. We would then make our way to a man-made concrete bridge that crossed the span of the creek.

This man-made structure acted like a dam at

this part of the creek. It was about two feet in width and approximately fifteen feet long. It wasn't completely solid because water was able to run under the structure. From the vantage point of standing on this dam, you were looking at the spillway coming from the other side of the interstate.

    The spillway appeared like two huge square eyes looking back at you. It was a long time before we ventured into the tunnels. Very little water would make its way through the tunnel and into the creek during normal conditions. When we had heavy rains, it created two miniature water falls as the water cascaded out of the tunnels. On the left side of the creek as you looked upstream was more of the rocky shore. We seldom wanted or needed to go on that side. The right side was a more prominent, desirable location. It was a huge rock formation, made smooth by years of water running. Sometimes it would be dry and other times it would have a few inches of water on its surface.

    We couldn't wait to drown a worm, or a piece of bologna, to see if it was possible to catch fish in our creek. Bait in hand, we set off with our fishing gear to give it a try. We raided our refrigerators to come up with acceptable bait. It would usually consist of a piece of bacon or bologna, though when desperate we would use bread or any other morsel. We were not beneath using Spam, Vienna sausages, salami, a slice of cheese; anything to get a bite. We became very good conservationist, wanting to spread the day's fishing bait out as far as possible. Running out of bait meant the day's fishing expedition had to end.

I don't recall if it was the first cast, or drop as it might have been, that resulted in a fish, but it didn't take long. THERE WERE FISH IN OUR CREEK!!! We could not believe our luck and good fortune. We could actually go to the creek, fish, and catch something. Life is good!

We quickly found out that if you dropped your bait straight down beside the man-made dam, there were fish waiting for a feast. It was like taking candy from a baby. And to top it off, you could even watch the fish fighting over which one would bite the bait. As the bait neared the opening under the structure, the current would push it slightly under the dam, and bam, a bite.

Boys will be boys and we crammed to get the ultimate fishing spot. We repeatedly tangled our lines trying to place the bait within biting distance of the fish. On many occasions, we hooked several fish at the same time. The size of the fish didn't matter at all. Most of the fish we were catching were pan fish, about three inches in length, barely able to get their mouths around the hook. The creek was not a stable environment for the fish because the water level fluctuated so much. I don't think the fish had time to mature to larger sizes, but occasionally we would catch a biggun' pushing five inches long.

Over a day's time we would "fish out" that wonderful spot under the dam. We must have pulled out everything that called that place home, some of the unfortunate (or dense) ones twice. Usually the bait would run out before the fish, but when the fish under the dam stopped biting and bait remained, it called for finding another fishing spot.

We tried the conventional method of just throwing the line in the middle of the pool of water with very little success. To a group of young boys, you've got to understand that if you have to wait until the bait drops all the way to the bottom, fishing is slow and you need to look for a new spot.

On a day when the water was slightly down, we made our way to the right side of the creek. This was the part that was one solid boulder, made smooth by the water. Behind this part of the creek was a bluff of about six feet, a wall of dirt with small brush growing at the top and a few roots of struggling trees hanging on.

We slowly made our way out to the edge of the rock. At this part of the creek the water was about three feet deep. Unlike the dam fishing, it was not as easy to see the bottom and maneuver the bait. So we would place the bait on the edge of the rock and slowly move it out until it fell off the edge and down towards the bottom. The rock we were standing on actually jetted out into the water and created a shady overhang for fish.

Again we found success. There were fish here too, and they were just as hungry. These fish were slightly larger than the ones we were catching under the dam. Now we could actually spread out a little and have less tie ups.

One day when the water was lower than normal, we could see to the bottom. We quickly noticed we were not alone. A massive turtle was living under the ledge along with the fish. We could only see the head and a little bit of the body. The head was huge, probably four inches long and three inches wide, easily the size of our fists. We surmised it must be a snapping turtle, very capable of biting our limbs off and not letting go until lightning struck.

Of course, just like the snake episode, our curiosity overcame our fear. We decided that the turtle could be caught just like the fish. We did not have success in this venture. My guess is that fellow had been around for a long time and knew what was going on. He was wiser than the fish and ignored our repeated attempts at hooking him. His presence did keep us on our toes and out of the water.

The second fishing hole we discovered was downstream from our usual entry point. This section of the creek was the widest part we knew. It was probably 30 to 40 feet wide at this section. The water was about 18 inches deep and very smooth and slow moving. The floor of the creek in this section was void of almost any rocks. Huge trees on both sides of the creek caused this segment too rarely, if ever, see the sun. Though the water was still in motion, it looked more like a smooth pond that a moving creek. It was a beautiful sight and probably deserved better treatment than it got from our group.

One thing that made this part of the creek a little less attractive than it would have been otherwise was one of the houses that bordered the section. This house had roughly ten dogs fenced in the back yard very close to the edge of the creek. These dogs did not appreciate us being in the same vicinity as they were and made it known. It sounded as if they were ready to tear us apart and if we were just passing through this part of the creek, we did so as quickly as possible.

The good news is that if our target was this particular section, the dogs would eventually wear themselves out and lose interest in our presence. As we became more comfortable with the persistent barking, we would sometimes bark back or try to splash water on the dogs. This was probably not a good idea in case the dogs ever found a way to escape their confinement.

There was a huge rock located just inches from the bank directly below the center of the caged dogs. This rock was big enough for three of us to stand atop of and tall enough to sit on the bottom and still have a dry top. I don't know why we decided we would drop our fishing lines there, but low and behold, yet another success. There were fish under that rock, too. These fish were even smaller, about two to three inches in length, but a fish nonetheless; and attached to our fishing poles.

    It must have looked hilarious to see a group of boys crowed on the only rock in sight, fishing straight down under that rock when there was all that beautiful water to fish. But we went were the fish were and they just happened to be located under that rock. Those dogs continued to believe they were going to receive a fish treat at anytime.

    The third and final fishing spot we found in Dry Creek was actually a string of three spots. The area was in a totally different location than the first two. We entered at the normal spot and just headed straight forward, climbing over the embankment on the far side of the creek, crossed about a 10 foot piece of land, and then make our way through an area we called "The Falls".

    Then we climbed a fifteen foot hill and made our way to the third fishing hole. This part of the creek had huge boulders placed randomly in the creek. The water made its way around these boulders in very small, quick moving streams. It appeared that these boulders were pushed around by big equipment sometime in the past.

    We would hop back and forth until we made our way to the other side. This was flat land with tall grass growing. We walked upstream about 15 feet to our destination. We called this spot the "Brim Hole". This was the first place we found that called for actual fishing. The creek was about three feet deep and very slow moving. It was approximately ten feet across and had a drop of about two feet from the bank to the water.

To fish at this location, we actually had to cast our lines to get to the fish. These fish were the biggest yet. They were average sized brim, much like you would catch in a lake or pond and there were bunches of them. This was overwhelming; we were doing some real fishing and didn't need to depend on any adults to get us to the fishing spot. There was also plenty of room on the bank for us to spread out and not tangle our lines.

Farther upstream was what we referred to as the "Bass Hole". This name came from the fact that one of us caught a small bass there once upon a time. This part of the creek was even wider and deeper. It was also canopied with beautiful, large trees that grew up and over the water, creating a tunnel-like covering over the creek, while still allowing enough sun through to make it pleasant. The roots of the bank side trees were exposed and added to the uniqueness of the area.

We didn't fish the Bass Hole as much as the Brim Hole because fishing was slower and the walk was farther. Although this spot yielded bigger fish, we were more excited by constant rewards than waiting for the elusive big one. My brother Ray fancied this place more than the rest of us. He must have been the one to catch that initial bass.

The third part of this trio of fishing spots was

the "Catfish Hole". We never caught a catfish at that spot, but the name kind of went along with the other two and we could always hope. It was much like the Bass Hole but less productive. It was also a longer walk, so we seldom made our way up that far because it meant passing other productive fishing places too enticing to pass up.

This series of stops in our creek world just never felt the same as our special spots along the main creek. I think the lack of familiarity with the nuances that came with the area caused this feeling. It almost felt like we were visitors in this area while we were at home in our normal places.

Though we occasionally saw various other types of wildlife, the final creatures we saw on a regular basis were tadpoles. While we would occasionally see the tiny variety of tadpoles often found in small pools of water like bird baths, the more commonly seen type at our creek were the big bullfrog tadpoles. We happened upon these guys most often in the slow moving waters near the caged dogs. These tadpoles were huge, about three inches in length and a good inch in width.

We found the tadpoles lying on the rock less bottom of the creek, wavering slightly with the current. They were very easy to sneak up on, but not as easy to capture. We were unable to use the bucket method we used on the minnows due to the openness of the area. This would be a hand to hand contest. Tadpoles used their large tails to move, wiggling them back and forth to propel forward. Even though they were not half as fast as the fleet minnow, tadpoles were still elusive.

Our choice of attack was to get as close to the tadpole as possible, kneel down as far as possible, and place our hands into the water. Ever so slightly, we moved our hands towards the target. Our hands were cupped to form a dome to place over the tadpole. When we got to within inches of the tadpole, we would quickly trap the fellow against the bottom. If we aimed slightly in front of the target, our chances were greatly enhanced.

If you trapped one, you knew it. These guys were thick, slimy and had some weight. We immediately wanted to watch as they developed into frogs. There were days when we would catch upwards of one hundred. We then hauled them home and waited for the great transformation from tadpole to frog.

We placed the bucket full of tadpoles in the shady area between the out building and the honeysuckle hedge. The tadpoles were at various stages of development, from full head and tail, to partial back legs, to four complete legs, to some who had already lost their tails. It was amazing how quickly that bucket grew algae. Within a couple days, the entire bucket was green, smelled nasty, and needed to be changed.

We were unsure what tadpoles ate, so we gave them a little bit of everything. Surely they ate pieces of bologna and cheese sandwiches. For a long time they continued to mature, some beginning to look very much like frogs.

Unfortunately, somewhere along the way, lack of nutrition, air, or clean water got to the tadpoles. Another thing we failed to consider was that the tadpoles would also change from breathing with gills to breathing with lungs. Our bucket did not allow for the newly forming frogs to breathe using their lungs.

On one of our daily checks of progression, the bucket smelled rancid. You could smell the bucket long before you could see it. What was once a bucket of promising frogs was now an amphibious morgue. Every one of the tadpoles died and we were reaping the aroma of decay. Great ideas don't always equal great success, and we seemed to prove that over and over.

One of the most unforgettable things I remember about our creek frolics was the famous rescue. One day we were on our way to fishing hole #1 just under the interstate. We had our equipment in hand and were ready to start another great day of fishing. When we arrived at the creek, we found it much lower than normal, with many spots completely dry. We made the hike across the creek bed and onto the dam to find a horrific sight. The creek was almost totally dried up except for a two inch pool of water about five feet in circumference. Within this pool were nearly one hundred fish, many clinging to life, others already dead.

We had no idea what to do. Not only were we not going to fish that day, our fishing spot was gone and the fish we were to catch were dead or dying. I don't know who receives credit for coming up with the idea, but we decided we must do everything within our power to save these helpless creatures and our fishing future.

We didn't have the bucket we normally took with us to the creek. We sent Ryan off on his bike to fetch it from home. He quickly jumped aboard his bike and took off, returning very quickly with the bucket. We filled the bucket with creek water and started scooping up the fish and throwing them into the bucket, trying not to include the dead ones. We salvaged several small containers that could hold water and filled those up as well.

When we had saved every fish we could find to save, we decided that the best place to relocate these guys behind the caged dogs. We took our buckets and containers and headed towards our bikes. Do you know how hard it is to try to peddle a bike carrying a bucket full of fish and water? The fish that were splashed out sure understood the difficulty. We were having a horrible time trying to relocate the fish to their new home. Finally we had to ditch our bikes and carry the buckets running.

We traded off carrying the heavy bucket and frequently switched hands in order to save them from being permanently damaged by the handle boring into our skin. We slowly made our way to our destination. We poured the contents of the containers near the rock that the other fish had made their home. Many of the fish did not survive the journey, but I'm glad to say that some did because of our hard work.

Fishing hole #1 took a lot of time to recover from the drought and the emptying of its fish. Knowing how seldom water actually made it through the spillway made it even more amazing that fish returned at all. We felt on top of the world for our efforts that day. Having to walk all the way back to retrieve our bikes was a small price to pay for that incredible feeling of success.

We had several special places we liked to visit at the creek and most of those places were given names. One of those places was "The Falls". This was a beautiful area of the creek and held plenty of adventures for us. It was actually a branch off from the main creek. It consisted of several small falls of between six inches to a foot until you came to the main falls. This area had a drop off of about four feet and was extremely wide. It was crescent in shape and very jagged. The water was usually barely more than a trickle as it came spilling down to join the main creek. The sound of all the water splashing was fascinating and the view was splendid. Tall trees created a canopy over the creek which allowed only a few rays of sunshine to make it to the ground. Fallen tree trunks, huge boulders, large pools of water, and dry areas spotted the falls area.

To get up the four foot rise to the top of the falls was a challenge, unless you took the easy way out and went around the edge. We would place our hands on the top ledge and pull up just as hard as possible. The slippery rocks made this even harder. To top it off, getting up dry was almost unattainable. We would often make the trip from top to bottom a race, which also up the likelihood that someone would take a spill. A spill in the regular creek would get you drenched. A spill at the falls would get you wet and injured.

Though we were tough on each other and took every chance to razz one another, we also knew how to lend a hand. If someone looked like they had spent all their energy and still couldn't make it up, we would give a yank or a shove, whichever was needed, so we could all be atop the falls together.

Wildlife was not as prominent in this area. I guess minnows and tadpoles didn't like the idea of falling four feet onto a hard rock. While there were crawdads to be found, the swifter current kept down those numbers as well. Small snakes dotted the rocks like they did under the smaller falls in the creek, but they seemed to disappear when we came close.

Once we were on top of the falls, there were three places to go. We could head upstream to the "Holes", go to the steep hills off to the right, or head left towards "Gilligan's Island". Most of the time we just spent some time in and around the falls and then headed back down. Getting back down from the falls was much quicker, but boy could it hurt. We would jump down onto the rock below, creating a big splash as we landed.

An area just to the side of "The Falls" was "Gilligan's Island". This place was very unusual in appearance and a blast. It was an offshoot from the falls and virtually a big mud slide that landed in a three foot deep pool. Years of running water had smoothed the "slide" so much that it was like a slide you would find at a local swimming pool. The water was a little warmer here due to the heating power of the sun on water that didn't move.

The pool was surrounded by very high dirt walls, reaching approximately eight feet high. Once you slid down the mud slide, you were totally encircled by those walls. At the far end of the pool, water would seep through an opening in the bowl. For some reason, there was a small fence erected across the opening. Debris that would float into the pool would pile up against the fence creating a damming effect made a deeper pool.

The only thing that would drain the pool would be a big rain storm, strong enough to push the debris through or over the fence. This would ensure that the water remained fresh and clean.

One of the fun games we played at "Gilligan's Island" was King of the Mountain. While it was fun to slide down the natural slide, it was also a blast to climb back to the top. Not an easy thing to do on slick rock and mud. Add to that some friends who were ready to push or pull you back into the pool and you had an all out free for all.

This was one of the few places at the creek

were we would actually take off our shoes. The bottom was void of rocks and the mud felt "cool" to our toes. The freedom from shoes just added to the joy. Many a "three hour tour" occurred on this Gilligan's Island.

One of the scariest situations that we encountered at the creek happened when heavy rains sent the creek over its banks. The water was extremely muddy and even had white caps. It seemed to be moving about a hundred times faster than normal. It was hard to recognize our usual stomping grounds beneath all the water. When the creek became this strong, it was impossible to play in except for throwing sticks in to see how far and fast they would float.

Little Tim was there with us that day to see the swollen creek. The rain had not even stopped, but we had heard it was something we must see. Tim could not have been more than six at the time, but as usual, he was hanging with the big guys. This was probably one of the reasons he became such a superb athlete.

When we arrived, there was a crowd of people interested in the rising creek waters. The majority of those present were the home owners whose property bordered the creek. They were watching helplessly, hoping they would not soon be enduring flood damage to their property.

We watched in awe as our creek turned into a thief, grabbing everything on the banks and taking it downstream. The noise changed from its normal pleasant ripple to an intimidating roar.

Large branches and fallen trees rushed downstream as if meager toothpicks.

Downstream from our normal entry point was a retaining wall, built to keep the creek from spilling into that resident's home. It was about four feet tall and usually did its job. There was a buckeye tree located right at the edge of the wall. We thought that the buckeyes would bring good luck if you rubbed them, so we often kept one in our pockets. Those buckeyes also provided great ammo to throw at each other.

We went to the retaining wall to get a better look at the raging water. The creek was almost level with the wall at that time. Tim ventured off to the edge of the wall, just a few feet away from us. The next thing we knew Tim slipped into the roaring creek. He fell feet first into the creek and was trying desperately to hold on to anything. He somehow managed to grab part of the wall to delay his trip down the creek. Luckily at that instant, David was able to grab his brother. We all helped in pulling the crying Tim ashore as a crowd gathered.

I'm not sure what the outcome would have been had we not been able to reach Tim. However, I think this made us respect the creek and its power more than ever. We conveniently failed to share this experience with our parents for fear that we would be banished forever from the creek. We've caught many fish in our days, but I doubt there was ever a bigger catch than Tim during that close call.

Another episode happened on a bitterly cold day in the dead of winter. It had been an abnormally cold week and we were out of school due to snow and ice. Ray and I attended Gateway Elementary, a Nashville public school, and the Lewis boys attended St. Joseph School, a private catholic school. We always waited nervously by the television to see if Snowbird was going to announce our school's closing for the following day. Snowbird was one of the local channel's winter weather mascots. St. Joseph normally closed whenever Metro Nashville School's did, but until both schools were announced closed, we weren't certain of a vacation.

Luckily for us, Snowbird had given us the day off and, even at this time of the year, we found ourselves at the creek. While most of the creek continued to flow during cold weather, the portion behind the caged dogs occasionally froze. When we arrived at the creek, we were ecstatic that the creek was indeed frozen over.

This wide, slow-moving part of the creek looked like a huge skating rink, glistening in the sun. The ice was an inch thick and totally solid from one bank to the other. We didn't own ice skates but sneakers worked just as well. There was no way we were staying off that ice. We had a ball sliding all over the frozen creek that day. The ice was see-through and you could watch the water flowing underneath. We laid down on the ice and looked for minnows, crawdads, and tadpoles making their way under the ice.

We started a hockey game using one of the ever present buckeyes. The neighbors must have had a good laugh watching us slip and slid all over the ice that day. We were getting our money's worth out of this snow day. CRACK! What was that noise?

It was as if the creek had enough of us playing and decided to end the fun. As we stood on the ice, small cracks began to form under and around us, playing a cruel game of tease. We tried, without success, to outrun the breaking ice!

One by one we fell through the ice into the freezing water. The initial shock of the cold water took our breath away. Luckily, our lives were not in peril in the shallow water, but nonetheless, it was shocking. The ice broke off in huge pieces, reenacting what ice bergs breaking off from glaciers must look like. Much like swimming on a steamy day when the water is cold, we soon became used to the freezing water, or at least tolerable of its temperature.

We turned our bad luck around and soon decided to break the remainder of the ice. We marched and stomped atop the ice, breaking it into a thousand pieces. I remember taking the sheets of ice and skipping them across the water like rocks. We even rode some of the larger pieces all the way to the bottom like surfers.

Little did we know we would soon pay for staying in the frigid water too long. When we arrived home and striped off our wet clothes, boots, and socks, we found our feet an intense shade of red. They were numb to the touch but didn't stay that way for long. As the blood started to pump and feeling returned to our feet, the pain was severe. Our feet were on fire and only an unbelievable amount of rubbing, stomping, and warming by the fire returned them to normal. I guess we were lucky we didn't suffer frostbite or hypothermia.

One adventure that we were part of occurred near "The Falls" though we were not actually in the creek's waters. Between the Falls and the Holes was dry land that went from flat forest type landscape to a steep hill that had a flat road type surface on top. At the top was a long, straight stretch of land that appeared to be an old road, not used in many decades. Where that road may have led remains a mystery. This area was very dense with trees and shady year around. During the summer months we would ride our bikes up and down the hills, usually pushing the bikes up the hill and roaring back down only to find out that trees made good breaks.

During the winter this area was a great sledding spot. We would lug our sleds from home to the creek and make our way across to this favored location.

Though the ride was very short, it was extremely fast. If we weren't careful at the bottom, because of the steep slope meeting the level landing, we might find ourselves continuing the trip without our sled. The front of the sled would dig into the ground, causing the sled to make a sudden stop. The momentum of our bodies would continue on, sending us head over heals across the land.

A game that evolved as we raced down the hill was King of the Hill. Anybody sledding down the hill became free game or targets for those at the bottom or on their way up.

As a rider passed, it became our goal to jump onto the sled and knock that person off. The ultimate achievement would be to not only knock the driver off, but to ride that same sled the rest of the way down.

From the opposite perspective, sled riders would try to take out as many climbers as possible. Taking a sled to the shins doesn't feel good to state the obvious. By the end of the day, sleds were usually tossed to the side and an all out pile up occurred as we simply ran up and down the hills to the point of exhaustion.

The creek was a place we loved and made many memories. I can't imagine there being a better place for boys to romp their summers and weekends away. Luckily, I had plenty of friends and a brother to share the fun and the laughter. The good Lord must have protected us from harm many times as we pushed the limits of safety over and over.

Chapter 2
School

Gateway Elementary School sat at the top of Monticello Avenue in the heart of Gateway Subdivision in Goodlettsville, Tennessee. Goodlettsville is located on the northern edge of Davidson County, home of Nashville, TN. The school was built with white brick with the occasional off color brick and had blue and light orange panels bordering each window. The front entrance had metal lattice work that integrated a few educational symbols, numbers, and letters. The right front of the building was a bank of cafeteria windows. These windows ran from three feet off the ground to the top of the building. The building was an "L" shape lying on its side from the front office. You could stand at the intersection of the two hallways and see almost the entire school. Because of the lack of space, only Kindergarten through Third Grades were housed in the building. Grades four through six were schooled in portables behind the main school building.

To the back right of the building was the famous playground court. The court was asphalt with yellow markings all over its surface, from a kickball field in one corner to the exercise circle in the opposite corner. Four square boxes could be found painted in several spots on the court. This is where PE started every day the weather cooperated. Adjacent to the court was a playground that included monkey bars, chin-up bars, a climbing tunnel and swings. There was also a huge plot of land that encompassed two backstops. To the left of the school was another huge piece of land that sloped down from the school all the way to the bordering fence at the far end of the property.

    The setting of Gateway Elementary School could not have been more perfect. Sitting in the middle of a subdivision that was home to almost entirely young families, it was truly a neighborhood school, with most children simply heading out their front door and walking to school. Two buses did take a group of students home and cars would pick students up every afternoon in front of the building.

    I began my years at Gateway Elementary in Mrs. Teft's Kindergarten classroom. It was located down the hall that ran straight from the front door. It was almost directly across from the library and the only classroom on the middle hallway. It had two windows that had a wonderful view of the promise land, the playground.

One of my recollections from Kindergarten class was sitting in the listening center with my newest buddy, Kenny Watkins, listening to *Yankee Doodle Dandy* over and over on a record player through headsets. We sang so loud that the teacher had to repeatedly ask us to quiet down or leave the coveted center. I also recall rest time. We used the same blue and red mats that can be found in most kindergarten and preschool classrooms today. My spot was against the wall, under the clock, not far from the classroom door. I enjoyed playing a game at the end of rest time each day. The goal was to act like I was sleeping so I could be the last one up. I don't remember what the benefit was to winning this game, but it sure was fun. I guess it was just my competitive juices building for later life. The biggest disappointment of Kindergarten was that my best buddy, David Lewis, was in the other classroom. This was the only year that we would attend school together. He would go on to attend St. Joseph's, Father Ryan, and Madison High School.

First grade was located just around the corner from my kindergarten class. My teacher was

Mrs. Finley. I remember crying on the first day of school that year. I was very quiet about it and took my seat on the carpet with the other kids, but none the less, I began crying.

   I quickly came to love Mrs. Finley. I remember thinking how tall she was and how beautiful her face appeared. She always dressed so pretty and smelled so nice. Her face seemed to glow under her reddish-blonde hair. I became very comfortable with Mrs. Finley and flourished in her classroom. She was able to teach and remain in control without raising her voice or embarrassing any child. I felt safe and always wanted to please her.

   I had developed many friends by first grade, and the majority of those friends ended up in class with me that year. Scott Jarrett became one of those close friends and we spent almost every year together in school through Junior College.

   First grade became the year of the chicken pox. It seemed like every day, someone else came down with those itchy bumps and disappeared from school for a week or two. Our art project repeated itself over and over during the outbreak. We made houses for our classmates who were stricken with chicken pox. This was great fun and I'm sure appreciated by those unable to come to school.

Mike's 1st Grade Class at Gateway

During PE that year, many of the boys had their shirts off during free play that followed our daily lap and exercises. Our classmate April wanted to know why she couldn't take her shirt off, too. Coach Clements, our PE teacher, got into a conversation with April I'm sure she had rather not be having with anyone. I do remember that by the end of Physical Education class that day, April's shirt was off and she loved it. At that age, the boys could have cared less.

Mrs. Vaughter was my second grade teacher. Her classroom was located down the other hall, at the far end, on the left. I remember thinking how sweet she was and how bright her clothes were that she wore. In particular was a light blue suit that she wore often. It made her eyes shine like no blue I had seen before. Again, almost all my close friends were enrolled in this class. Not only did I adore Mrs. Vaughter, I was so excited about not having the other second grade teacher. I had heard at home that she had actually tied my brother Ray to a chair. Now, did he deserve it? Probably so, but I still didn't want any part of that teacher or her classroom. The other classroom was located directly across the hall from ours and I always tried to take a peek into that classroom to see who was being tied up.

We were about as far as you could be from the restroom in Mrs. Vaughter's class and still be in the building. In fact, to get to our classroom, you had to go down about six stairs. We took advantage of that fact during our restroom breaks. In most boys' restrooms, you will find toilets and urinals. In the boy's restroom at Gateway, there was a "Super urinal". This gadget was one long trough with water constantly dripping down from a pipe.

This urinal became the site of one of the most ferocious competitions in the school building, from second grade to when we became to cool to join in the fun in the upper grades. We would line up on one end of the urinal and see who could pee to the other side. We experimented with angles, force, and projectory. Occasionally a slice or hook would send someone running to the sink to wash off their clothes. Modesty was not an important part of a second grade boy's life.

I started to realize in second grade that school

came pretty easy for me. I had a lot of friends, a lot of success on the playground, and made really good grades. Something else I began to notice was that I always seemed to be paired or grouped with other kids who did well in school. We were called blue birds, eagles, or group number 1 and appeared to do harder work than some of our classmates. I remember having a proud feeling in my stomach that I was being successful in school.

    Success was never more apparent than on Field Day that year. Field Day occurred near the end of school each year and was a competitive event in which students competed against their classmates in four physical activities under the direction of PE Coach Clements. Parents, grandparents, aunts, uncles, younger siblings, and most of the neighborhood would show up for this grand event. Coach Clements would use her megaphone to announce events and you even had to report to the scorers table before and after each event. There was usually a dash of some sort, a crab walk type event, some kind of throwing event, and balancing something on your head. I'm not sure what the four events were during my second grade year, but I do remember the outcome. I won first place in all four events. I couldn't believe it and I still have the ribbons today to prove it. As Mrs. Vaughter passed out the ribbons in class at the end of the day, I remember having mixed feelings. I was so proud of winning, but at the same time, I felt bad for the other boys in the class. This was in a time before everyone had to be a winner or they would be scared for life. First, second, and third place were the only awards; there were not participation ribbons given.

The next year was third grade in Mrs. Wilson's class. Mrs. Wilson wasn't as flashy as my previous teachers. She was very plain in dress and appearance, but her heart was far from plain. I could tell she loved to teach, loved her students, and had a special style. She was very quiet most of the time and didn't see the need to put on a show. I remember Mrs. Wilson making it seem okay to not care about all the outward things that students can sometimes long for or brag about to classmates. She made it cool to just be yourself.

A new part of school life began in third grade, girls. Yeah, they had been around, but up until this point, they were more of a necessary evil or hazard to be avoided. Leah Bass was the girl in my class that caught my eye. She had medium length, light brown hair and a beautiful, dark complexion. She was about my height and very slender. She could even hold her own on the kickball court and was in the high achieving group. Leah rode the bus to and from school, which made her more mysterious. I guess this was the first time I actually checked the YES box on that famous note.

For some reason, crayons quit being just for coloring and soon became a source of alternate entertainment, not to mention a big mess. We decided it would be fun to carve crayons into little shavings and store the shavings in our pencil boxes. The bigger you could create the shaving without breaking it, the better. I'm not sure how this came about or what the intended purpose was, but it was a mess. Soon we had splotches of crayons on everything: clothes, desk, books, chairs, and especially the floor. Needless to say, Mrs. Wilson, nor Mr. Eddie, the custodian, appreciated our crayon art.

Third grade was also a special year in that we learned to play recorders. These are the little black "flutes" that are still played in schools today. I remember learning the fingering to *Joy to the World* and sharing that song at the annual Christmas Coffee. Schools did not have music teachers while I was growing up, so it was up to Mrs. Wilson to find time for music in our schedule. After lots of practice and screeching, you could actually envision what the song was supposed to sound like.

I also remember singing lots of songs in the classroom. The songs *"I've Traveled this Wide World All Over"* and *"Get On Board"* still ring in my head today. We used the turn table to spin the records and went to town. The words were written in a music book that we took off the shelf any chance we got.

Third grade was also the year of multiplication tables. I was great at Math and this was another chance to shine. We were able to move at our own pace and I busted out of the blocks. I couldn't wait for Mrs. Wilson to call me to the round table so I could pass the next level. It was a fierce competition between friends to finish the levels first. Not only did accuracy matter, speed was of the utmost importance. Like most students, sixes and sevens caused me the biggest problems.

I still remember standing in the half-bath of our Friendship Ct. home with Daddy learning and practicing the multiplication facts. He was really good at math and knew a really cool way to remember the nines. It turned out that every answer, when the individual digits were added up, equaled nine. How cool was that? My dad had to be a genius. I quickly finished my times tables after that hint and flew all the way through the twelves, wondering why we didn't continue to the thirteens.

The television in our third grade room served two purposes. One was to instruct us in handwriting. I must have written an encyclopedia of words with my finger in the sky, copying the lady on the television. How did she get letters and words to come out of her finger tips and magically be written in the air? I struggled to stay attentive during this program and that is probably the reason my handwriting is often non-legible today. Watch, think, and pretend apparently was not my style of learning.

    The other use was to watch the occasional television program, usually The Electric Company. I'm not sure if we watched this show as part of our Science curriculum or just to give the teacher a break, but it was awesome. Hearing that wonderful music rising to fever pitch and watching that huge wall falling down to reveal the secret word of the day was fantastic. The theme music still rolls through my head today.

Mrs. Riley was my fourth grade teacher. She appeared to be a giant and her huge afro must have added another eight inches to her stature. She also happened to be my first black teacher. In fact, she may have been the first black person I had met besides Mr. Eddie, the custodian. I don't remember having any black classmates up to this point, no African-American people attended our church, nor do I recall coming across anyone who didn't look just like me around town.

    I shared a birthday with Mrs. Riley, which I thought was a really cool thing. Every time June 8 rolls around, I still think of Mrs. Riley. Fourth grade meant moving outside of the school building and into a portable. We were in the portable closest to the playground court. For the first time, weather had more of an effect on me than just arrival and dismissal from school. Every time we had to enter or exit the school, you had to consider wearing your coat or not, depending on the time of year.

I think being in a portable was a huge benefit. It seemed as if we were in our own little world of learning and became a close knit group. It also minimized the distractions that are often happening in the hallways of school.

Mrs. Riley's 4th Grade Classroom, Gateway Elementary School

One of the first rules that Mrs. Riley relayed to us was the emergency restroom rule. We would take regular restroom breaks throughout the day and you were welcomed to ask to go to the restroom at anytime. However, if you couldn't wait to ask, or Mrs. Riley's answer was no, there was the "no accident" clause. If it was an emergency, you went, no questions asked, no punishment acquired.

Though this seemed like an open invitation to take advantage of, it was never an issue. However, this policy came to fruition one afternoon on a typically quiet school day. Roger Ross suddenly rose from his seat and busted out the door, jumped passed the steps to the ground, and hightailed it into the building. It took us all by surprise, including Mrs. Riley. Roger had to go, so Roger went. I bet only three seconds elapsed from the time he started getting up until he disappeared inside the building. It took a lot of nerve to do that, but it also took guts to return and face all those staring eyes. Mrs. Riley stood by her word and never said a thing to Roger.

Roger was also the focal point of another incident in Mrs. Riley's room. We were putting up some decorations around the room one afternoon. We were entrusted with some staplers to help in our task. The inside walls of our portable were covered with wood paneling. A staple would easily and securely go into the wood and made hanging up items on the walls effortless.

To begin decorating, we flipped open the stapler so it could be pressed flat against the wall. We had gotten about half way through the project when Roger let out a howl the office probably heard. He had stapled his thumb instead of the wall. That staple went all the way into his thumb on both sides of his fingernail. So, for the second time that year, Roger flew from the classroom into the building, this time headed for the clinic. It was both hilarious and scary at the same time. We were worried about Roger until he arrived back in the room reasonably okay. The conversation turned to wise cracks and replays of the event, each one more animated and boisterous.

Fourth grade was the first time we changed classes for specific subjects. I was assigned to Mrs. Mitchell's room for Reading. Mrs. Mitchell's class was located in a portable about two doors down from our own. This was great news for me. For the first time in my schooling years, the majority of my friends were located in the other class. Luckily, they stayed with Mrs. Mitchell and I joined them for Reading.

Two things come to mind when I think of Mrs. Mitchell and her class. The first was that we learned how to crochet. I'm not sure if this went along with a certain story we read or if Mrs. Mitchell just thought we should learn to crochet. I enjoyed it and most of us produced a nicely crochted place mat. I chose Dallas Cowboy colored yarn, complete with silver sparkles embedded within the material. I can still remember trying to manipulate the yarn and those darn long sticks.

The second was that Mrs. Mitchell made us use our given name. I had gone by Mike my entire life. When she said I would be Michael in her class, I didn't think it was that big of a deal. Most people knew my name was Michael and it was a fairly common, innocent name. About the worse that happened with Michael was kids would say "Michael, Michael, motorcycle" or "Michael, Row the Boat Ashore". However, when I went to write my name on my paper, I realized I didn't know if it was spelled Michael or Micheal. I went with Micheal, which proved to be wrong. Luckily, only Mrs. Mitchell and I knew of the misspelling.

While attending Gateway, I was involved in speech classes. I called my brother Ray, Way, and was unable to pronounce various other sounds. I would leave the classroom approximately once a week and spend thirty minutes working with a speech pathologist on the pronunciation of those troublesome sounds. This usually occurred in a closet or some other tiny area due to lack of space within the school.

Many speech problems are connected to hearing difficulties, so I was consistently having my hearing evaluated. If I had a dollar for every time I raised my hand when I heard the beep, I'd be a rich man. To this day I'm tempted to raise my hand when I hear a beep.

Though my speech gradually improved through the years with the help of the therapy, while reading aloud during class in Mrs. Riley's room, I pronounced something incorrectly. A few of my classmates giggled, including some of my best friends. This happened sporadically and I don't remember it bothering me. However, Mrs. Riley was not going to allow this type of behavior in HER class. She exploded! I thought the roof of the portable was going to blow off or the paneling on the walls would splinter. This time the ringing in my ears wasn't from the hearing test, it was from the booming voice of my teacher and protector. She came down on the guilty full force, letting them have it with no holding back.

I was whirling about within my feelings as I sat in my desk witnessing this outburst. On the one hand, I was horrified that my friends were in trouble because of me (or so I thought). However, the other part of me was totally enjoying the onslaught they were enduring as I silently cheered Mrs. Riley on. It must have lasted a good five minutes, but seemed more like an hour. The strange thing is that after she was finished, she quietly took a seat and said, "Go ahead and read Mike". I never heard another snicker while I read nor was there any backlash on the playground. Mrs. Riley, my birthday buddy, became an instant hero.

The highlight of the year for the boys in the class came just before Christmas vacation. We were seated at our desks working when someone came knocking at our door. The next few moments went by in slow motion. In walked Terri Sue Page, a new student to Gateway Elementary and our class. She was absolutely the most beautiful human being I had ever seen. She had long, shiny blonde hair that bounced as she walked, beautiful blue eyes that you could nearly see through, and she was shorter than me, which was very important to me at that time. She had on yellow overalls with a green checkered shirt underneath. Every boy in the class set with our eyes wide open and our mouths hung low. It took awhile to take our eyes off Terri, but then we started taking peeks at each other, congratulating ourselves on our unbelievable luck. Terri and I would be "boyfriend/girlfriend" off and on through the years but more importantly, great friends.

Fifth grade brought a new experience to my schooling. I was in a split grade class. I had no idea that students in different grade levels were ever placed in the same class. Mrs. Shelby Callis had fourth and fifth graders in the same classroom, and we had moved back inside the school building. Almost every one of my friends was in the class and some of my favorite fourth graders. It was a great year, the best yet. Mrs.

Callis was an extraordinary teacher, and even I could recognize it as a fifth grader. She pushed us to our limits and made us produce our best work.

We put on a Dental Health puppet show while in Mrs. Callis' class. She got Mrs. Winters, our librarian, to work with us. We made sock puppets and performed in front of many of the younger classes. We had great fun and often had to catch our breath from laughing as we read the script behind the curtain. I remember playing several roles in the play, including a dentist. The bad part, in my opinion, about the role of the dentist, was that I had to stand out front and didn't get to "hide" behind the curtain where all the fun was occurring.

Mrs. Callis served as the unofficial assistant principal under Mr. Davis. This meant that we behaved in class or there would be dire consequences. We usually towed the line except for Shay, the class clown. He was the funniest person I had ever been around. He was tiny, had a shaved head, and always dressed disheveled. He turned many a routine day into a comedy show. Much like the old cereal commercial that announced "lets get Mikey, Mikey likes it", we could always poke, prod, and/or tease Shay into doing some of the craziest, most insane things in the classroom. Shay seemed to be up for anything. Unfortunately for Shay, Mrs. Callis didn't always appreciate his humor, though I did witness her struggle not to laugh at some of his foolishness.

Gateway always held a talent show near the end of each school year. One Sunday morning, in the back of the "Showcase" section of the newspaper, I found the song "Blue Jeans". Scott Jarrett and I decided we would perform this song during the talent show.

The idea started as we lined up on the wall after lunch each day, waiting for our teacher. As we stood against the wall, Scott and I would sing the song, each day adding a twist or some extra little sound effect. We thought we were pretty good and wanted to share our talent with the world. One day as our class was on its way outside for some extra recess, the call was made over the intercom for talent show contestants to come to the cafeteria to try-out for the show. We nervously walked to the cafeteria and took our seats.

As time passed, I became more and more nervous and I think Scott did as well. I'm not sure if it was the talent that was being displayed, the fact that the rest of our class was playing kickball, or that we were just plain chicken, but we hightailed in out of the cafeteria before we auditioned, never looking back at our chance for stardom. To add insult to injury, Mrs. Callis said we had made our choice and we would not be involved in recess that day.

As Scott and I sat and watched the talent show, with Billy Paulie belting out "Let There Be Peace On Earth", a sixth grader pounding out

"Wipeout" on his drums, and a fifth grade girl twirling batons to "Do, Run, Run, Run", we knew we were out of our league and had made the right choice. I still can sing every word of "Blue Jeans" today and I'm positive Scott can too.

    School lunches have historically been made fun of by students. I'm sure not all school cafeterias have the same quality of the food as the Gateway cafeteria, but it was some good vittles. I took my lunchbox to schools on some days, but never on Monday or Fridays.

    Monday was pizza day, my favorite. You would get a slice of square pizza and fries. I loved both and became known as the French Fry Monster, a parody to Sesame Street's Cookie Monster. I earned that moniker by devouring my fries and then begging for everyone else's around me. It became a game and soon I seemed to be eating about ten servings of fries every Monday.

    Friday was Hamburger day. Hamburgers, of course, came with fries also. This was the most popular day in the cafeteria and the line would be longer than usual. Mrs. Jones, the lunch lady, would carry her big ladle around, making sure we were behaving. When she hit that thing on the table, it got everyone's attention fast. Not following the cafeteria rules would get you a seat by yourself. Being one of the only times of the day when you could talk freely with your friends for an extended amount of time, you definitely didn't want to be sitting by yourself in silence.

I remember being busted along with my friends for loud and excessive talking during lunch. The punishment was to copy an entire dictionary page during lunch while in isolation. I remember thinking I'll take care of this punishment in no time. However, I didn't realize the huge amount of information on a single dictionary page. We were required to write every single word, symbol, and dot. Lunch went from being a great time to a time of dread. Eventually we would rejoin our class at the table, but with a much clearer knowledge of correct, lunchtime behavior.

   One of the most remarkable things I recall from lunch time centered on Roger Ross. Milk cartons were the choice of drink in the cafeteria, not that there was any other option. Roger could drink an entire carton in about two seconds and usually without spilling a drop or spewing the contents. I have no idea how he did this, but we would all give him our own milk cartoon to show off his magic.

   Sixth grade would be my last year at Gateway Elementary School. I was finally the top dog (or Gator), oldest in the school. I was placed in Mrs. Marcin's class, a brand new teacher to the school. We were in a portable to the left of the school, directly behind an unused portable and diagonal from the other sixth grade class. Mrs. Marcin was the first teacher I remember who talked about her personal life and family. She had twin boys that the class heard about frequently. I have many wonderful memories from sixth grade.

Part of Physical Education class in the sixth grade was square dancing. Though we had long gotten over the "girls are gross" thing, boys were still uncomfortable, to say the least, with dancing with the ladies and having to hold their hand. Coach Clement taught us individual steps involved in square dancing and we soon became able to string some of the steps together to form a short dance. This actually was fun, and when she put on the music with the real square dance caller, we moved like we knew what we were doing. Of course we had to be careful to not look like we were having fun.

We figured this would last a few weeks and we would be back to the favored kickball and football games. What we didn't know was that this square dancing thing would conclude with us in full costume performing for the entire school and community. UGH! Coach put us into squares consisting of four couples. As couples were assigned, my top choices were quickly assigned to my buddies. Terri was placed with Troy Denton, Amy Campbell was with Scott, and Tandy Hankins was paired with Kenny. That left my partner as Dawn Steakley. Dawn was one of the smartest girls in school and a great friend. The problem I had with her as a partner was that she was at least a foot taller than me, and that was before she puffed her hair for the big day.

The day came and we appeared in our western wear. The boys had on plaid shirts with matching handkerchiefs tied around our necks, our best jeans, and boots if we owned a pair. The girls had on huge, frilly dresses that matched their partner in color. Dawn and I were assigned red; and it matched the color of my face.

Once the music got underway, all was fine. We circled, bowed, and promenaded around that kickball court something fancy. The younger students came to watch and were captivated with the twirling and the up-tempo music. We were grade school stars and we knew it. Our square actually won the competition and thus ended our square dancing careers as champions.

Mrs. Marcin's Sixth Grade Class; Gateway Elementary

With square dancing complete, we could go back to more serious activities. Kickball was king at Gateway. The court had a painted field and was the perfect size for a game. We played every chance we got and looked forward to the traditional year-end kickball tournament. Many lunches were used to create the perfect kickball line-up, defense, and strategy for that day's match.

I remember making up a line-up one day at lunch, fully prepared to use it that day at PE. Coach Clements got wind of our shenanigans and made us run the line-up backwards for the rest of the week. I went from clean-up man to mop-up kicker. Coach's move didn't stop us from making the perfect line-up, but it sure made us nervous every time we did.

It came time for the yearend showdown on the kickball court between six grade classes. Who would be this year's Michael House, who had actually kicked a ball onto the school building from the kickball field and was an instant hero? Who would make a forever remembered catch or throw out a runner at home?

It would be our class versus the other sixth grade class, Mrs. McConnell. Mrs. McConnell had actually hurt her back earlier in the year and Mrs. Davenport became the teacher, but we continued to call the class Mrs. McConnell.

The instructions from Coach Clements were to pick five girls and five boys to represent the class. The way the players were chosen was left entirely up to the class and their teacher. This was the long standing tradition that had been used since the tournaments began. I remember voting in the portable classroom late one Friday afternoon. Mrs. Marcin was at the board talking us through how we would conduct the vote. I remember being nervous about not being chosen to participate. What if I was left off the team? What if I had to watch from the sidelines?

My nerves were put at rest when my name was added to the roster as boy captain. Terri Page was named the girl captain. We had picked the team and there were not any surprises. After seven years of playing kickball almost daily, everyone knew who the best players were in each class. We were ready to put together a line-up to destroy the opponent.

One thing we didn't count on was an uprising from those who weren't included on the team. Timothy, a boy who rarely joined in on many kickball games, decided he and the others should be included in the tournament. I think this came about more as an "I'll show them" campaign than a real desire to play. Tim never played when given a choice during PE. A discussion was held between the teachers and Coach Clements and the decision was made to let everyone play.

Our chosen team was devastated! We felt we had the best 10 player team, but weren't nearly as confident when everyone was included. The other class had more good or average players than we did. The tension in the classroom was excessive. Those that had made the team were furious that everyone was allowed to play, and some of those added to the team after the rule change were being snotty about the whole process. We were far from being a unified team, more likely to battle each other than Mrs. McConnell's class.

The tournament was a best of three format, meaning you had to win two games to win the championship. We thought long and hard about how our line-up would look. We decided to spread out our most talented players, rotate between boys and girls, and use the very best players every fourth kicker, our clean-uppers. I ended up kicking about sixteenth in the newly revised line-up.

Our strategy was an epic fail. We got pummeled, the score long hidden in the depths of my brain. And to top if off, one of their strongest boys crushed Terri with the ball as she ran towards second base. Even though she was called safe by Coach for unsportsmanlike conduct, it stirred up things as we rushed to protect our player. It wasn't just any player; it was Terri Page they were messing with that day! Order was temporarily restored, but we wouldn't forget. Unfortunately, one of our guys decided the best way to deal with the situation was "an eye for an eye" and he pummeled one of their girls at first chance. Again, things became tense but Coach Clement handled the situation very skillfully and the game was completed.

We returned for Game 2 fired up, ready to defend our honor and Terri, and won the game. We changed our strategy and decided to top load the line-up in hopes that the better kickers would get more chances. It worked and we got some surprising defensive plays from some of our weaker players. Mrs. McConnell's class quickly spread the rumor that they allowed us to win so we would get to play a third game. Of course only they know the truth, but I don't think eleven and twelve year olds would be able to control their competitive juices enough to blow a game on purpose and allow us to come within one game of the championship.

Game three was a sight to behold. The entire school came to watch the spectacle. Students lined the court down the foul lines, three or four deep. Having been a spectator for six years, it was hard to believe it was my turn to be in the limelight on the field. The game was tight. The scoring went back and forth and both classes were playing great. The low scoring contest did not end in our favor. We lost 4 to 3 in a defensive battle. We were devastated, never imagining that we could really lose the series.

Upon returning to the classroom, Robbie Sechler kicked the trash can, denting it in several places, unable to control his anger in losing. Blame began to be placed around the room and a very unsportsmanlike atmosphere developed. "If only you did this" or "If Tim would have kept his big mouth shut" were some of the things being voiced. Finally, Mrs. Marcin had to have a long classroom talk about appropriate behavior and what being a team really means. It took awhile for the feelings to calm, but they did and our class slowly returned to its normalcy.

Throughout the year, Mrs. Marcin had awarded good behaviors and excellent work with tickets. Tickets came in denominations, much like money. They could be earned with great school work, leadership, following directions, or behaving appropriately. I stored mine in an old peanut butter tub that I kept in my bedroom at home. It was yellow and had red writing on the outside. It also had a white, plastic handle used to carry it around. I remember Mrs. Marcin giving each of us a ticket worth fifty for Christmas.

We knew we wanted to accumulate as many tickets as possible, but we weren't sure of their purpose. It turned out that we were going to have a year-end auction. Parents and others had donated items that we could bid on with our tickets. It was a blast and we got many great things with our tickets. Not only was it a wonderful motivator, it was also a teaching tool. With this process, Mrs. Marcin taught responsibility, keeping up with the tickets, and economics, assigning a value to objects. Some of the first items auctioned went for huge amounts while more sought after later items were won for a fraction of the cost. I later used this system in my own classroom.

    Sixth grade was the first year you could play in the band. The band director, Mr. Doster, would come to Gateway a few times a week and conduct band class in the portable nearest the court (Ms. Riley's previous portable).

    I decided I would play the trumpet like my brother and father. My parents were able to find an instrument for me to use. I only lasted half the year before dropping out. Due to lack of talent, dedication, and desire, I became a band flunky, not to mention wasting my parent's money. Many of my friends followed suit and dropped out also, but John Moore continued to be in the band throughout high school.

    Teachers did their own art classes in those days. When we became six graders, we learned that Coach Clements would be doing some of our art instruction. We would explore the art of pottery. It was a new experience for all of us and great fun. She had set up shop in Mrs. Riley's old portable, no longer needed to hold a classroom. This was the same portable used for band class. We molded blocks of clay into various cups and bowls and then used glaze to create designs. The odd thing about glaze was that you really couldn't tell what the finished product would look like until it came out of the kiln. Regardless of the color it was suppose to be, all the glazes seemed to be clear.

    The last part of the process was baking the pottery in the kiln. Coach warned us that if we allowed air bubbles to be present in our creations, we risked it blowing up and destroying itself and damaging those items around it. The kiln was located in my old speech room, the closet. You could tell when Coach had it turned on by the odd smell that crept throughout the building.

We anxiously waited to see how our self-made pottery would turn out. My piece came out like I imagined it would, but I also remember the disappointed looks on the faces of those that were damaged or destroyed by those nasty air bubbles.

I'm not sure how the next story developed, but we found ourselves in the middle of a basketball game at Goodlettsville High School, where most of the six graders would be enrolled for the following school year. During PE, Coach Clements formed two basketball teams of six graders of near equal talent. We practiced for about a week and then played a game in front of the entire school. We knew the kickball tournament was on the horizon, but this came as a wonderful, unexpected surprise. We used the two goals on the opposite ends of the court from the kickball court. Students were seated so close to the court, you had to be careful not to step on them when doing a lay-up or bringing the ball inbounds. The goals on the court were uneven and the rims were bent, but we thought we were NBA stars playing in front of a sold-out crowd.

Only when the game concluded did we find out that this was only a practice game for the real, upcoming contest. We would be the half-time entertainment at a Goodlettsville High School basketball game. My team wore orange Tennessee Volunteer uniforms while the other team dressed in the black and gold of the Vanderbilt Commodores. We sit on the top row of the bleachers at the high school and waited nervously for our debut. This was big time in our conceited minds.

Our team lost as both teams flew up and down the court, expending nervous energy, and showing very little talent. Randy Stivers was the only player who would have a high school basketball career as he suited up later for the Madison Rams. I would come back to coach middle school basketball on that same court with much better results.

It was Field Day time again at the school. We were eligible to compete in all four events if we wished. I ended up winning the first three events of the day, a dash, a crabwalk, and a balance race. The fourth and final event was a two-person event called the *salt grinder*. You were to chose a partner, hold both hands, and twist yourselves round and round towards the finish line. You only competed against other boys, so that meant you had to hold hands with a boy, and as six graders, we were much to cool to do that, especially in front of a large crowd.

However, Coach convinced us to race and Scott and I won the event. That meant for the second time in my Gateway career, I had swept first place at Field Day. Oddly enough, I had the same mixed feelings when it was time to pass out the ribbons as I did while in the second grade.

School work continued to come easy for me, except for the issue of spelling. In sixth grade, instead of being placed in a high group or given alternate assignments, for the first time the high achievers took a different course. A group of students was sent to Mrs. McConnell class to take 7th Grade Math. Our heads swelled as the books were passed out. We were doing the same math as the kids at the junior high school. In reality, I didn't notice a big change in the work, but the fact that the teachers thought I was worthy of this class made me very proud and I strived to prove them right.

Mr. Eddie Walton was the custodian at the school and had been the whole time I was a student. Mr. Eddie was one of our favorites and we loved to pass him in the hallways. One thing we all wanted from Eddie was his Vanderbilt Football programs. He went to all the games and returned to school each Monday with the coveted program. It became a game to see who could persuade Mr. Eddie to give him the program.

Mr. Eddie sure seemed to have a sweet heart and worked very hard. Thirty years later, as I stood in the office of a school as principal, a very familiar face came in to pick up a child for a friend. As I stared into his eyes, somehow he seemed familiar. It was Mr. Eddie, hair graying and the pounds packed on, still showing the same smile I remember in the Gateway halls.

As a sixth grader, I was eligible for the School Safety Patrol. A dozen or so students were chosen to help with school arrival and dismissal. You had to be a neighborhood kid who walked to school, keep up good grades, have parent permission, and be deemed responsible enough to handle the job. Coach Clements was in charge of choosing and maintaining the School Patrol.

I was selected as a patrol boy and proudly wore my banana looking yellow hard hat and belt/sash combo, badge included. Many of the patrol kids would help with loading cars in front of the school and the others would walk to the corner intersections to help walkers cross the road. I was stationed at the corner of Monticello and West Monticello Avenues. I carried a long pole with a yellow flag on the end that said STOP on both sides.

It was my responsibility to be the first one to the corner to assist in making sure students crossed the corner safely. We were well trained and did our job proudly and took it seriously. We were the precursors to today's Patrol Ladies and Men. We didn't realize what a hazardous job we had and what a huge responsibility we had undertaken. I'm glad to say that we didn't lose or injure one student under our care.

Six graders were also ushered into the school chorus, under the direction of Principal Billy Davis. Unless you were excruciating to listen to, you became part of the performing chorus. Tryouts consisted of singing a repeated line from a patriotic song back to Mr. Davis. Luckily, we "tried out" by alphabetical order and very few people were left to hear my nervous attempt at singing. If you were truly a dreadful singer, Mr. Davis would shake his head and point towards the back door. My good buddy Robbie Sechler hated the thought of being in the chorus and purposely bombed the tryout and was given the heave ho by Mr. Davis. Robbie held his head high as he waved to all of us and went on his way.

I can still remember some of the songs we sang. *You Light Up My Life, Pick Cotton, It's A Small World, All the Gold in California, You Can Sing a Rainbow,* and *This Land Is Your Land.* Mr. Davis made it fun to be a part of chorus and played both the piano and the guitar. I was even part of a trio, with Scott and Troy Denson, which sang the opening of *All the Gold in California.*

We sang at the annual Christmas Coffee and were able to go to Whites Creek High School to sing in the Elementary School Chorus Festival. We sat in the bleachers and were directed by Fran Powell. This was huge! Mrs. Powell was the lady who appeared on all the television shows that taught us how to sing as we sat in the classroom through the years.

I loved to have fun at school and had many friends, but I was still a very shy child, especially towards the teachers and other adults in the building. While sitting in the back of class during Science one day, as far from the door as possible, I had to use the restroom urgently. Both six grade classes were wedged together as the teachers team taught the topic of the day. I was too scared to ask permission and not willing to invoke the "Roger Ross" clause. I couldn't hold it and drenched my pants that day.

I remember wearing my green jeans and just soaking them through and through. Even after the accident, I was too embarrassed to tell anybody. We left for PE and I remember running my laps in those wet pants, wondering if anyone noticed the huge spot or smelled me as they passed. By the time school was over for the day, the pants were dry and I didn't even tell my parents. Believe it or not, the same thing happened the following day.

During my sixth grade year I attempted my first try at being an entrepreneur. During the yearly Scholastic Book Fair, I noticed one of the biggest selling items was pencils with furry heads on the eraser end. If you twirled the pencil back and forth in your hands, the fur would spike out, leaving the character with a nice shaggy hair style.

I decided I could make these novelty pencils just as good and possibly make some money. I convinced Mom to take me to the craft store where I bought the needed supplies. I purchased pencils, fuzzy fabric, glue, beady eyes and I was open for business.

I made a few examples and took them to school to tempt my classmates into making a purchase. The orders flew in and I found myself spending most the evening making fuzzy headed pencils. The only "sticky" point was the gluing of the fabric to itself.

The entire process was only about five steps. I would cut the fuzzy fabric the desired length and width, staple the starting edge to the pencil, wrap the cloth around itself, and then glue the ending edge down before gluing on the beady eyes.

The problem became getting the glue to stick to the fabric. I remember trying several types of glue and attempting several different ways of getting it to work. Nothing seemed to work until we tried a second staple at the end. This was the answer and sales continued to be brisk in the beginning.

However, having a limited number of classmates hurt sales. Very quickly, everyone either had bought a pencil from Scholastic or me, or simply didn't care to have one, and business dried up.

Having money became more and more important as I grew and this was one of my first attempts to make my own. Birthday cards, the Tooth Fairy, and report cards had generated money previously, but this undertaking opened my eyes to capitalism.

I recall some other ways I made money during my early years were pulling bagworms off the front scrubs for five cents each, taking back glass soft drink bottles to Kroger for the refund, and mowing the lawn. However, after deciding to mow the front yard in no particular pattern, zigzagging everywhere, that chore became "on the house" for awhile.

As a yearend treat for finishing our elementary careers, our teachers organized a trip for us to Opryland. Opryland was a country music themed amusement park in Nashville and a blast for children of all ages. We met at the school on a Saturday morning and headed out to the park. I was currently "going" with Terri and couldn't wait to spend the day with her and my friends. In fact, I told my baseball coach I would not be at that day's game due to the class trip.

I was a part of the 11 and 12 year old Major Giants, playing out of the Dixie Youth League at Moss-Wright Park in Goodlettsville. We were competing for the championship and had a big game that day against the rival Braves. One of the problems I encountered was that Randy Stivers, a Giant teammate, and John Moore, a Braves player, were also going on the trip, but planned on returning in time for the game. Coach Charlie Bryant didn't appreciate my lack of commitment to the team and told me so in front of the team after a Thursday night practice.

Still, I stayed with the plan and spent the entire day at Opryland with Terri and friends. We had a blast riding rides, eating treats, and just hanging out. Late in the day we returned to school. I walked very slowly home, tired from the day of excitement. I cut through the normal yards and headed towards the Lewis house to climb the fence into my yard. Julie Lewis, the oldest Lewis child and only girl, saw me and asked if I was headed to the game. I told her that it was probably over by now. She told me that the games were hours behind schedule and it wouldn't even be starting for another hour.

    I took off running towards home as fast as I could. I arrived at the game before it started and thought I had been blessed with a stroke of luck. Wrong! Coach was infuriated with me anyway and I went from being the starting second baseman to a seldom used bench player. I understood in a way, but held to my choice to celebrate with my friends.

    I still think the decision to stay on the class trip and not return to the game cost me a spot on that year's all-star team. I had made previous all-star teams, but this was different. Goodlettsville was hosting the Dixie Youth World Series and the host team received an automatic spot in the tournament. I would be a fan at the World Series and not a player. What I think may be the most telling part of the story is that Coach Charlie started me at second base for the championship game. I guess in his eyes, I learned my lesson just in time to help us win the championship.

Chapter 3
Sports

Regardless of the time of year, we found some type of sport to play. We played countless games of wiffle ball or tennis ball in the Lewis backyard. We nicknamed their backyard Little Wrigley because of the love the Lewis family had for the Chicago Cubs and their home Wrigley Field. The most used field had home plate next to the house, so the house acted like a backstop. First base was a large tree near the neighboring Hunt family fence line, second base was an in-ground rock, third base was a smaller tree near their out building, and home plate was a well worn dirt spot near the water spout.

We pitched the ball from about 35 feet away, where another spot was worn in the grass. Most games were two on two contests. Ghost Runners were used when both players were left on base. We tried to keep up with when ghost runners scored or were forced out, but it became almost impossible.

The fact that the first base line ran parallel to their next door neighbors, the Hunts, was a huge problem. Many balls were both hit and thrown over the fence into their yard. This doesn't seem like a very big deal. We all hopped fences like they weren't there, going from yard to yard with ease. However, the meanest Cocker Spaniel on the planet lived in that yard. Ryan, Tim, and I were all bitten by that hated dog at one point or another. I was bit on the tip of my thumb as I sprinted back towards the fence with a wiffle ball. Tim had it the worst when he was bit on the face by the mangy mutt, barely making it over the fence before the attack. As the dog aged, it became less active and ignored us for the most part. We made many quick darts in and out of the yard retrieving the ball with one eye on the destination and the other on that wretched mongrel.

Beyond second base was another fence, the home run fence. This fence separated my yard from the Lewis yard. Thick hedge, a club house and ricks of firewood became secondary obstacles to hitting a ball over that fence. In the corner where the fences met was a fierce, thorn bearing bush that injured many players retrieving hits. The smaller you were the better chance you had at getting to the ball without drawing blood.

The third base border was the fence of the neighbors on the other side, the Pruitts. This fence seldom came into play. Unlike the Cocker Spaniel, their dog, Snowball, loved visitors. That was what comprised Little Wrigley, the wiffle ball center of our universe.

The wiffle ball of choice was the one that only had holes on one side of the ball. The best of the best was the actual *Wiffle* brand ball. You could make that type of ball do tricks on its way to the plate. It relentlessly changed shapes as it was thrown and hit and kept the pitchers and fielders on their toes. Every time a slight variation happened to the ball, the way it moved changed. What it took to throw a looping curve last inning might sail up and into the batter the following inning.

Trying to hit balls that moved multiple ways made us all develop great hitting eyes. We all had success transferring that talent from the backyard to the Little Leagues. As mentioned previously, I think Tim and Ryan benefited the most by playing with and against the older boys.

One difference in the game of wiffle ball and the game of baseball is getting people out. Instead of throwing balls to bases to get a force or tagging a runner out, in wiffle ball it's much more simple, and painful. The rules allowed runners to be beaned with the ball at any range. Not only were you out, you were hurting.

Somewhere along the way, I decided to keep stats of our games, complete with thoroughly typed box scores. In my busy little head, I would remember everything that happened during the game. When we finished the game, I would run home and sit down at Mom's manual typewriter. I would type down each game's score, stats, and highlights, trying to make it look just like the box scores in the daily newspaper. I kept up with season stats as well as records. I loved it and even kept the scorebook for my son's Little League teams.

When the Lewis' bought a huge shed and placed it in the backyard, we moved our field. The building's side became the backstop. This allowed us to move from beneath a canopy of trees and out into the open, thus allowing for more homeruns. The Hunt fence, home of the Killer Cocker, became the homerun fence. It was much more acceptable to chance teeth marks retrieving a homerun than a foul or overthrown ball. The major drawback to this setup was that the outbuilding's base was about a foot off the ground, allowing many wild pitches and foul tips to roll far under the building. It meant finding a long limb or sending little Tim crawling under the building to retrieve the balls so the games could continue.

An alternate wiffle ball game came about as a result of not always being able to get four people to play. We called the game *Strikeout* and it was a pitcher vs. hitter contests. The game was very simple. The goal of the pitcher was to strike out the batter. The pitcher was the umpire and called balls and strikes. A few times we tried to draw a strike zone with chalk but, because of the different sizes of the batters, it always created more problems than it solved.

The batter's job was to not strike out. If you hit the ball you received points. Grounders counted one point, fly balls three, and line drives were worth five. A batted ball had to go past the pitcher in order to count and if the pitcher caught a fly ball or line drive, it was an out.

To up the difficulty of the game, we pitched from only about twenty feet away. The normal Little League mound distance is 46 feet. That distance didn't give you much time to react. Throw in the fact that the ball was probably moving in a spastic manner, it was extremely tricky to make contact with the ball.

When Moss-Wright Park hosted the Dixie Youth World Series in 1980, they sold and gave out Styrofoam baseballs with the Dixie Youth logo imprinted on the side. These could not be thrown very hard, but boy did they move in the strangest of ways. Unlike the wiffle balls, there was no way to tell where this ball would go. And every time the ball was hit, it would compress just a little smaller. If we were fortunate enough not to lose the ball, it would shrink to the size of a golf ball as it was hit over and over.

I've mentioned two hazards that we faced while playing backyard ball; the Killer Cocker and the thorny bush. There was yet another hazard in the backyard: dog piles.

The Lewis' had two large dogs growing up; first Charmane, a black lab and then Dusty, a grey Weimaraner. Both dogs loved to hang out with the guys. Dusty could even climb the fence to come over to my house. However, they did leave big piles behind.

The obvious risk was stepping in a pile. Doing so stirred up the stench and stayed in the treads of your sneakers for days. The less obvious danger was stepping in a pile as you were running the bases. If you stepped in a pile while hauling full speed, it often meant a sudden spill. Those piles where slippery, stinky, and continually multiplying.

Little did we know that there were other baseball/wiffleball games going on around the neighborhood. We were approached by a group of guys two streets over on Gates Avenue. They had formed a team and challenged us to a game. To top things off, they played with real baseballs and had a yard *almost* big enough to play.

We all played organized baseball with the local league but we never had enough room to whip out the hardball in the backyard. Our windows appreciated us staying with the plastic wiffle balls. We accepted the challenge and set a date for the big game.

Our first jobs were to pick a name and come up with a uniform. We chose the team name Sox for one reason only. It was short and would cost the least money to make. We dug out old white tee-shirts, got on our bikes, and rode up to McHenry Center, a local shopping strip. There was a business there which made shirts by using really big steam presses. We each had a uniform made with the word Sox diagonally down the front in black lettering. The large numbers for the back were too expensive so we rode home and used a black marker to make our numbers.

We showed up to play with our gloves and bat, looking every bit like a ragtag group. We immediately realized we had a predicament. The other team had a catcher with catching gear. Nobody on our team had ever caught and we didn't have the first piece of catching equipment.

Our opponents graciously agreed to share their equipment and we each gave catching a shot. I don't remember much about the game but it became apparent that; like us, they didn't really have enough room to play baseball either. As far as fun went, this was boring compared to our typical fast-paced backyard duels. The pitching was bad, the catching was shoddier, and the game soon ended from lack of interest.

We gave this neighborhood baseball league idea one more shot. There was yet another team ready to play a couple streets over. We arrived in their back yard to see a much more suitable space. It looked large enough to play a game. However, the same boredom overcame us and a foul ball through the window of the house sent us scurrying, thus ended our association with the Gateway Backyard Baseball League.

Another baseball game that we had a lot of fun playing was *hot box* or *pickle*. You needed a minimum of three people to play and more was desirable. Two people wore gloves and covered two bases as fielders. Everyone else became a base runner. The object of the game was to get from one base to the other without getting tagged out. This was done by timing the fielders' throws, taking advantage of errors, or sneaking back and forth while the fielders paid attention to the other runners. Each base stolen was worth a point.

Little did we know we were actually practicing many skills we would use later on the baseball field; sliding, throwing, running bases, tagging and many more.

To pep the game up, the fielders would tease the runners by throwing the ball high in the air or purposely dropping the ball. Fake throws were tried as well as other hidden ball tricks. Voiced enticements such as "chicken" or "bet you can't" really got the action moving.

Football was also a big hit in the streets and yards of Gateway subdivision. We spent hours throwing, kicking, and punting the ball back and forth on Kathy Avenue in front of the Lewis home or in Friendship Court. We loved to have contests to see who could punt the farthest, highest, or most accurate. David constantly won and became a kicker and punter in high school.

We loved to catch and throw sideline passes in the street. The street was the field and we intentionally threw passes to the edges to see if the receiver could catch the ball and keep both feet inbounds. The curb proved to be a superior tackler.

Another favorite was to carry the radio outside on Saturdays and mimic a college football game that was playing on the radio, usually Vanderbilt or Tennessee. We became the stars of our favorite teams and great actors at the same time. John Ward, the legendary voice of the Tennessee Volunteers, was mimicked over and over throughout the years. Some of my favorites were: *Touchdown Tennessee, First Down Big Orange, It's Football Time in Tennessee*, or the slow *5, 4, 3, 2, 1 Give Him Six.*

Besides our own yards, we turned yards into football fields all over the subdivision. The closest field to our house was the "Old Lady's" yard. She lived on the corner of Friendship Drive and Friendship Court. This yard was fairly flat and both wide and long. This was where we played when we just wanting a quick pick-up game. The most unique thing about the field was that it always had white dog poop here and there. I don't know what kind of dog does this or what causes this to happen, but it was always present and was rarely seen anywhere else. The "Old Lady" either didn't mind us playing or didn't want to waste her energy running us off. Looking back, I doubt she was more than fifty years old at the time.

Another favorite spot for football was across

the street from the Lewis house. We seldom saw the people who lived there, but the yard was very long, though sloping downhill. They did run us out of their yard once when they arrived home. We also had pickup games behind Kenny's house where hedges were the end zones, John Moore's house where the actual house was the out of bounds marker, at the school, in Tim Presley's front yard where the tree was in play, on lower Janette Avenue near the creek, in Randy Stivers yard even though his parents didn't allow football and Randy was always the first to quit, and even in our small front yard if needed but beware of sticky bushes.

Mike putting on his football tough guy look. Father Newel is in the background.

Most of the time we played tackle, though our parents discouraged it and school prohibit it. After we grew, we did go to a lot of two hand touch games when the collisions hurt more and the soreness lasted longer. The rules were always the same, regardless of who was playing or where the game was being played. Two completed passes equaled a first down, regardless of the yardage gained. You could rush immediately once every set of downs and had to count to three Mississippi otherwise. Kickoffs were always thrown and the receiving team had the option of calling "spot" pass. This was when the person catching the kick-off had the option of throwing a forward pass.

The quarterback started with the ball without a center being used and could call "shotgun" to move farther back from the line. The term "Shotgun" was made famous by the NFL's Dallas Cowboys, the favorite team of many of us during that time. The defensive would call whether a legal tag was made and all touchdowns counted seven points.

We loved to play *Pick up and Smear*. This is where whoever had the ball became the runner and the goal of everyone else was to tackle, or smear, him. There was no scoring, downs, or time limits. When a player was tackled, he simply tossed the ball away for someone else to pick up. It was a fun, though tiring game and pile ups were a must.

Probably the most fun we had on the

neighborhood gridiron was playing tear away football. We would all put on an old tee-shirt and start a game of Pick up and Smear. The difference was you had to tackle each other by pulling on the shirt. The idea was to completely rip apart the shirt. The winner was the last person having a shirt on their body.

    We reenacted the moves of the players of the day. Whether we were Billy "White Shoes" Johnson doing his fancy end zone dance, "Mean" Joe Green sacking the quarterback, Roger Staubach throwing a perfect pass, or Ray Guy punting the ball seeming forever high, we loved to play. Skirmishes occasionally broke out and sometimes someone would get angry and go home, but the game would always bring us back, ready to give it another go.

    Basketball was also a big hit in Gateway Town. We were fortunate enough to have a goal in our driveway. Daddy put in the goal for us to play. He actually had to chip away at solid rock to make enough room for a telephone pole to set. He then poured concrete in the hole to set the pole in place. That pole wasn't going anywhere and is probably just as strong and stable today.

    The big advance in playing basketball was when my parents had our patio paved. It was awesome. We now had a basketball court in our own backyard disguised as a driveway. The *thump-thump-thump* of the dribbling balls was non-stop and I'm sure the neighbors hated it as much as an irritating barking dog.

We had a blast playing games of one-on-one, H-O-R-S-E, Around the World, Lightning, Free Throw contests, half-court shots, 21, and all sorts or made up and altered games.

Everyone had their preferred spot on the court to shoot. Mine was the far right corner, right next to the grass and the gravel driveway. I could make shot after shot from that spot and put out many a challenger from there in a game of HORSE.

Every March we would play out the NCAA basketball tourney. We would play every game of the tournament over and over and then make up our own brackets. The games would be played to ten by ones and then we would pencil in the winner on the self-made bracket. I still remember trying to write on the paper on the concrete. It created a very interesting font.

Much like we did during football season, we would always turn on the radio and act out the SEC games that were being broadcasted. I was Tennessee Vol Dale Ellis many a night while David would be Vanderbilt Commodores Charles Davis or Mike Rhodes. Kentucky Wildcats Kenny "Sky" Walker and Sam Bowie were always the imaginary defenders as we drove for the winning shot.

One day we decided we needed a name for

our "team". Even though we never played anyone, we decided we were an unbeatable group. We decided on the name Strippers, after a "nothing but net shot", not a streaker, though I wouldn't be surprised it that added to the names worth. We used markers to create the shirts and wore then proudly.

Like the wiffle ball field, there were hazards on the patio basketball court as well. The one that came into play most often was the mud pit that always seemed to form underneath the basket. The pole set about three inches from the edge of the patio. We would often land in the grass after lay-ups, missed shots, or while taking a charge on defense. This wore out the grass and created somewhat of an indention.

Whenever it rained, it became a mess. The balls would constantly land in the muck. We would try to wipe the ball off in the grass, but it was never completely successful, and we would track up the court with mud. When one of us would land in the mud, it was even worse, and soon the entire court would wind up slick and dirty.

The other hazards had to do with things surrounding the court. There was a shed just to the left that had a very sharp corner. There were woodpiles that could scar us up and housed many wasps. The brick fireplace near the back could scratch a person very easily, and the gravel in the driveway, just off the court, could cause a tumble if you were not careful.

Daddy had a chalk line that we used to mark off different things on our basketball court. You stretched out the string, which was covered with blue chalk dusk, and "popped" it to mark the desired area. We marked off the foul line, the lane, hot spots for shoot outs, and other various things. By the time we moved away, I could even touch the net.

Basketball often moved inside, especially during extreme weather. The hoop and ball of choice for indoor play was Nerf. Nerf was a brand and the ball was made of foam. The goal had about a six inch circumference and was hung from any door. Attached to the rim was a very thin net that hung to tiny hooks.

Before we knocked out some walls in our Gateway house, I would hang the goal on the door connecting our kitchen and den. Dribbling was difficult with the foam ball but I did my best. Our kitchen was laid with shagless carpet of blues and greens that created fabulous designs and dampened a lot of the noise that I made by bouncing around.

I usually played alone on this court. I would either reenact games from the past, both my own and those I had seen on the television, or play along with the radio. Other times I would see how many free throws I could make in a row and try to do some nifty new move. As time went by and boredom crept in, shots began to fly off the wall, the refrigerator, or even any person who happened to be in the area.

The Nerf battles at the Lewis household were an entirely different story. The choice of courts there was their den, a converted garage and their gathering place. The hoop was hung on a closet door that was higher than most doors due to base of the door being a good foot off the floor. We battled over and over in that den, having a blast competing against each other. We would play one on one or two on two, depending on the number of players available. We pushed, tackled, and ran over each other turning our basketball game into a football type affair.

Many shots were taken from a prone position as we wound up smashed on the couch or the minimally cushioned floor. The great thing about the Lewis den was the very high ceiling. This allowed us to take long, arching shots from the entire room. The biggest draw back was the light fixture that hung down in the middle of the room.

That fixture was broken numerous times as we took careless jump shots from the center of the room. The part of the lamp that would break was the long, slender globe that covered the bulb. The routine never seemed to change. We would have a great game going on with ever increasing enthusiasm and effort. Then, all of the sudden, someone would jump up to shoot or attempt to block a shot and the glass would pour down.

I don't recall anyone being injured by the falling glass or the shards on the floor, but I do remember how the aftermath would go. Mrs. Lewis spent most of her time in the front living room and was oblivious most of the time to the damage being done in the den. However, Mr. Lewis, Adrian by name, Rock by legend, would blow his stack.

"How could so many boys be so stupid? If you'd use the brains God gave an elephant. I'll be (bleep) if you'll ever play ball in this house again.", and on and on it went. I was glad I'd be going home soon but felt sorry for the Lewis boys having to continue being waylaid.

We would lay low for about an hour and be back at it as soon as the chance arose and we felt we were safe. We took the game of HORSE into the Lewis household. We used every square inch of the den to create some ridiculous shots. We'd call "Nothing But Net", "Bank", "Backwards", and every other possible combination in order to pin a letter on the other guys.

The biggest neighborhood gatherings occurred around basketball. Guys from all over would converge on the asphalt basketball court of Gateway Elementary every late fall. We would chose up sides and play for hours. Most games went to ten by ones and you had to win by two. The winning team kept playing while the losers had to wait to be picked again. Nothing beats outside basketball with a gripless rubber ball, a chain net, and a bent rim.

John and Kenny considered the school their "home court" and were sharp shooters on that goal. They would spend hours shooting shot after shot, making the majority. The biggest draw back of playing at the school was the court's edge. The court was actually built up from the ground a good foot near the basketball goal of preference. Missed shots and passes routinely hit the edge and bounced away, down a small hill. This would cause a stoppage in the game as someone had to go retrieve the ball. Another drawback was not knowing who would show to play. Would there be enough to play, too many, people you'd rather not play with, or players too good or not good enough?

Mike, following a game of Junior Pro Basketball

I loved playing sports growing up, especially baseball and basketball. In the seventies, the beginning ages for organized sports were much older than they are today. I started playing t-ball at the age of eight. I was assigned to the Tigers and excited to put on the royal blue uniform.

The uniform consisted of a solid blue T-shirt without words or numbers and a blue hat, again without any type of lettering. We wore whatever type of pants our moms put on us. Some players wore cleats while some wore tennis shoes.

My parents were able to get David and me on the same team. This helped our parents with transportation to practices. It also helped me be more at ease knowing a teammate so well.

We played at Peay Park off Main Street in Goodlettsville. Peay Park consisted of three fields. The smallest field set at the far end of the park, up on a hill. This field saw many tee-ball games and most of the girls' softball games. There was no parking at the field and teams and fans had to climb up the steep incline to watch their superstar.

The middle field was for the big guys, a regulation size baseball diamond. It looked huge and was an awesome sight. I would later play high school baseball on that same field as part of the Goodlettsville Trojans.

The first field in the park was the showcase field. This is where the majority of games were held. This field had real dugouts that were five steps below field level. The dugouts were constructed of cinder blocks painted green. A chain link fence protected players in the dugouts from catching a grounder to the chops. A slanted roof kept rain from pouring onto the field.

This type of dugout kept fans away from the players and players away from the fans. Only four small cutouts in the end of each dugout made communication possible. The water nozzle inside each dugout was a huge hit.

This field had a huge grandstand on the first base side. This is where the majority of fans watched games. A small section of bleachers were on the third base side. Directly behind home plate was a building. The bottom floor consisted of a concession stand while the second floor consisted of the scorebook and scoreboard keepers. A plastic tube running from the press box to a hole in the fence behind home plate allowed the scorers to give baseballs to the umpires as needed.

Opening day was a big celebration and spotlighted all the teams and their sponsors. We showed up early in the morning dressed in our snazzy T-shirts and caps, proud to be Tigers. When the festivities started, PA announcers called out the T-ball Tigers and we marched out proudly to our designated spot. When all the teams were called, an overhead picture was taken from atop the concession stand and the season had officially begun.

We were very successful and won the league's championship. We played the Cubs in the championship game, facing their trio of Chris's, Chris Carr, Chris Vetetoe, and Chris White. They wore yellow T-shirts and caps and fought hard before succumbing to the Tigers.

I was slightly disappointed not to be named an all-star but apparently my name didn't start with the right letter. David, Danny, Duane, and

Derrick were named the Tiger all-stars and all were super players.

As a nine year old, I was to be a minor leaguer the following year. This would be kids actually pitching. I was assigned to the Giants and again would have David as a teammate. We wore blue shirts with red block letters spelling out Giants across the chest. On the back of my uniform, I sported the number 7. We wore white pants with a red, white, and blue elastic waistband and a red and blue stripe down the sides. Over white tube socks we wore blue stirrups and the cleats of our choice. Our caps were blue and had a red "G" outlined in white on the front. We were dressed like the big leaguers and ready for action.

Being a nine year old on a nine and ten year old team meant playing time was sometimes hard to come by. We struggled to win games that year, finishing with a sub-five hundred record. I shared playing time at second base with Bobby Bloodworth, a ten year old. As the season wore on, I earned more and more playing time as I proved myself a scrappy hitter with good speed and a good glove.

When you were picked by a team as a nine year old, you stayed with that team for four years, two in the minor leagues and two in majors. Along with David, several other Giants would become longtime friends. Randy Stivers from Gateway, Tim Fry, and Chris Carr formed the nucleus of our team for the next four years.

Quite possibly the most interesting story to come from my nine year old season had nothing to do with the baseball diamond. One of the greatest things about Peay Park was that it was located within walking distance of Dairy Queen. A periodic treat following a game was a milkshake from DQ, on the coaches tab.

There was a well-known, well-traveled short cut from the fields to the Dairy Queen. Just past centerfield was where the path began. Just a little way into the woods was a creek. To cross the creek, we would walk across a large sewer line. It was about a foot wide and easily crossed. Occasionally, someone would fall off into the creek, splashing everyone within range. The creek was only a foot deep, so the embarrassment did more damage than the fall.

On one of our post game trips for a milkshake, Randy decided he wasn't going to walk across the pipe. After much persuasion, Randy decided he would cross, but not by walking. He made the decision to straddle the pipe and pull himself across. This would have been perfectly safe and fine if the pipe had not recently been greased.

When Randy made it across, his white uniform pants were black. From his crotch to his ankles, the inside of both pant legs were covered in grease. His step-father, Wade Hunley, one of our coaches, blew a gasket. Randy would have been better off falling into the creek headfirst, a crawdad pinching his nose, and swallowing a dozen minnows than facing the wrath of Wade. I don't think his pants were the only thing that changed color later that day at the Hunley/Stivers household.

As ten year olds, our nine year old nucleus was ready to turn things around, and we did just that. With Tim manning third, Randy at shortstop, myself at second, and David at first, we comprised a very formidable squad. Chris was an excellent catcher and capable nine year olds manned the outfield.

The Giants steamrolled through the first fourteen games of the season undefeated. I went from being a scrappy hitter to one of the league's best. From our Little Wrigley wiffleball field emerged two talented hitters. As published in the local Goodlettsville Gazette, I finished third in the league in batting average behind former T-ball Tiger teammates Richmond Miller and Derrick West. My buddy David finished the year as the fifth ranked hitter.

With the league championship wrapped up by winning both halves, we went into our last game against the Minor league Tigers with only one goal, finishing the season undefeated. As we sat in the dugout waiting for the Tigers to finish their pregame drills, coach gave us our pep talk. He said to have fun, this is just icing on the cake. Another former T-ball Tiger had an alternate plan. Danny Smart pitched a great game and they played great defense, including a homerun saving catch in the outfield. The bottom dwelling Tigers had slayed the Giants, sending us to our only loss of the season.

Following the season I made the all-star team. We wore white shirts with blue sleeves and three blue stars across the chest. The pants were blue with white pinstripes and our caps were blue with a white "G" and stars. All the Giant regulars made the squad and we were joined by the best players from the remaining teams.

We played in the district all-star tournament hosted by the Greenbrier Little League. I saw some action at second base, but spent most of my time manning centerfield. We dominated the other teams and I made the tournament clinching catch on a fly ball to center.

After winning the district tournament, it was on to the Regionals. We were quickly eliminated by a team called Volunteer, based in the Tusculum area of Nashville. Though disappointed, that team was so much better than us it made accepting our defeat a little easier.

My Giant experience moved onto Majors as an eleven year old. The biggest change was not the league but the park. The City of Goodlettsville had annexed land from Sumner County and built a beautiful new park called Moss-Wright. The park consisted of an historical home, the Bowen-Campbell house, two adult softball diamonds, three baseball fields, a girl's softball field, two football fields, and lots of practice areas, playgrounds, shelters, and a walking trail.

We would be playing our games on fields six and eight in the quad. Each field had a grass infield, chain link dugouts, and a fenced-in bullpen. A large building placed right in the center of the quad served several purposes. The bottom floor consisted of a concession stand, restrooms, and field maintenance storage. The second floor was separated into four press boxes, each with room for a dozen people. From each press box you could announce the game, keep the scoreboard, and keep the scorebook.

My eleven year old year very closely resembled my nine year old year. This year's version of the Giants just wasn't very good. We had the same core group of guys but not many good twelve year old players. We struggled throughout the year to win games and were relieved when the season came to a close.

The up and down Giant roller coaster would continue the next year, my last before moving on to the big field. We added a player by the name of Johnny Drennen. Johnny was a natural athlete and gave us another exceptional pitcher. Although we didn't dominate like we did as tens, we were in a fight for the championship.

I was having a great year at the plate, but that would soon come crashing to a halt. That fateful six grade trip to Opryland was looming on the horizon and I chose love over baseball. Without discussing it with my parents or coaches, I chose to forgo an important game to spend the entire day with Terri Page and my Gateway classmates.

I was relegated to the bench for the remainder of the year, seeing only minimum late game action. However, I was reinstated as the starting second baseman for the championship game against the Braves and their fireballer Richard Adams. We won a very close game and received our championship trophies. However, even as a twelve year old boy, I recognized the hypocrisy of the coach in allowing me to start.

I wasn't named an all-star that year due to my late season decision and watched as Goodlettsville hosted the Dixie Youth World Series. Our boys put up a hard fight, proving the host team wasn't a pushover. We were eliminated with a 1-2 record and that ended another season.

The following week, I was enjoying my post-baseball season time at Pleasant Green Swimming Pool. After a day of fun in the sun, I came home and we had a message. The voice on the answering machine said I had made the all-star team that would try to play their way through the tournaments and join the Goodlettsville host team in the World Series. This was great except one thing. The first game started in about two hours. I got dressed, unsure of what to wear, and rushed down to Shelby Park in Nashville. I found the team warming up on the field, changed into the all-star uniform and manned second base. I don't remember much of the tournament, but we failed to advance and for the second time that summer, baseball was over.

I had a much more memorable start to my organized basketball career. We started basketball at the age of eight and played on nine foot goals. Goal extensions were hung on the regulation goals to make the lower, more reachable nine foot goals. I was placed on the gold team with eight other boys. Our uniform was a gold T-shirt with a black numeral, white short-shorts and yellow striped tube socks.

We followed the regular rules of basketball except for two distinctions, the lower goals and you weren't allowed to guard the other team until they crossed half court. I worked the second rule to my favor. Most boys at this age were not yet good dribblers I was one of the few exceptions. Due to many backyard battles, I possessed the hand-eye coordination to look up while dribbling and still feel and control the ball with my hand. Our plan was simple and very effective. I stood at half court and waited for the opponent to cross the line. Then while they were staring at the ball, or losing control, I stole it and drove for a simple lay-up. We did this time after time until blowout restrictions made us calm our defense down.

If the other team got past me, scored, or for some other reason made us bring the ball up court without the advantage of a breakaway, our offense adapted. Troy Collins was a good foot taller than anybody else on our team and most of the other teams. I would dribble the ball up court and keep dribbling until I could find Troy open or drive for a lay-up.

We were scheduled to have our pictures made after one Saturday's game. We won the game by the score of 35-7. I scored 31 points and Troy scored the rest. I remember trying to get other teammates involved in the game, but they simply couldn't score or didn't even care to touch the ball. The team picture tells the complete story. I am blood red with sweaty, wet hair; Troy is flushed and sweating, while the rest of the team looked like they could be playing their game after the pictures were taken.

My buddy Scott Jarrett was on that team that year. While a good backyard player, he struggled in games. Late in the season Scott had not scored a single point. His daddy promised him fifty dollars if he scored, regardless of how. Scott told me about the deal before the game and I promised to help. Once the game was in hand, I constantly passed the ball to Scott. He kept slinging up shot after shot but could not get one to fall. He never did get a score that year and the money went uncollected.

We played in the championship game against the white uniformed team. They had a sponsor on the front of their uniforms by the name of Randall Phillips Builders, a startup construction company. Phillips Builders is now one of the biggest homebuilders in the Southeast. As I looked at their line-up, it looked a lot like the t-ball team our Tigers had beaten the previous spring. They had the Chris connection, Chris Carr, Chris Vetetoe, and Chris White. Much like the baseball championship, we put it to them and took home the hardware.

I didn't know it at the time, but that would be the pinnacle of my basketball days. Never again would I dominate on the basketball court like I did that first year. The other kids' abilities quickly caught up to mine and I no longer had the edge. I played a couple of years for Cole and Garrett, the local funeral home, and a couple more for Dairy Queen before bowing out.

While playing for Cole and Garrett, a local restaurant decided to video tape the games, complete with play by play, and show the replay at the restaurant later in the day. The marketing idea worked and we all headed over to Mr. Gatti's to eat pizza and watch our sports debut. We watched intensely as our game was shown on the big screen for all the patrons to see.

The announcer did a great job, quickly nicknaming Tony Cantrell "hacksaw" after he committed two hard early fouls. The highlight of the broadcast came late in the game for me. I had hit a couple lay-ups and made a few foul shots, having my usual average day but nothing spectacular. In the waning moments I launched a looping, long-range shot from the corner with the defense bearing down.

Remarkably, the shot hit the bottom of the net. Though the shot was exciting enough live, the announcer added some pizzazz. I can still hear the words, "Westveer's shot from Demumbreun (a downtown Nashville street), nothing but net.

What a shot". This ended my career as a television sports star.

The neat thing about playing for Dairy Queen was that our coach was the owner of the local DQ. Tom Kominos was a great guy who wanted to be involved with his kids. He had two sons, Kenny and Dennis. Both of the boys played on our basketball team so it was truly a family affair. We were average at best, but when you add in Mr. Kominos' coaching philosophy, we really struggled to win.

We had ten boys on the team and Tom felt we should all play the exact same amount. Like most every ball team in the world, we had some good players and we had some not-so-good players. Regardless, we all played two quarters. The score of the game didn't matter; it was always one quarter in, one quarter out. Our record proved the longstanding belief that the more you can keep your better players on the court, the better chance you have of winning the game. When our best players went to the bench, the opponent's best players continued to play. It was frustrating at times, but not nearly as much to me as it was to David Lewis and his father.

Like the majority of seasons, David and I wound up on the same team. I loved to win, but David was intense, and he got that intensity from his father. Equal playing time for all didn't sit well with either father or son. I remember one game in particular we were hanging with a better team. Near the conclusion of a tight game, when most in attendance thought David and I should be playing, Tom stood by his guns. Adrian confronted Tom and didn't hold back. The fact that there was a crowd, including youngsters, didn't soften his words. After he said his piece, he took David and left, vowing not to return to his version of a debacle. It proved to be a half-truth. David would play again but Adrian never reappeared.

Following that lowlight was the season's highlight for the red cladded Dairy Queen squad. We were set to face Mark and Scott Jarrett and the undefeated Celtics, clothed in their replica Boston Celtic uniforms. This team was dominant, and seemed primed for a blowout win over the equal access DQers. Fate seemed to be on our side. Only eight players showed up for the game and as luck would have it, our best players were all present and ready to play.

We played the game of our lives and found ourselves in the middle of a barn burner. The game went back and forth and I remember seeing the panic in the Celtic players' eyes. They were stunned and growing less confident with every passing minute. The pushovers were pushing back. We pulled out the victory, sending the Celtics to their only loss of the season. I continued to play basketball for several more years, but my lack of size, and more importantly, talent, caused me to slide into the realm of mediocrity.

Chapter 4
Bikes

Bikes were vital to each of us growing up. We went from training wheels all the way up to ten speeds. Ray was the first one to have a supped up bike within the group. He had a shiny green five speed with a speedometer. That bike was breathtaking. Ray loved to set up jumps by placing old plywood on top of a piece of firewood. In fact, he got his CB name, "Puddle Jumper", from his love of jumping ramps on his bike.

My love for bikes started by watching Daddy ride his Schwinn bicycle. It was a black model that didn't have any frills, but it rode smoother than any of the other bikes we ever owned. I wanted to be able to ride like Daddy, so the bike adventures began.

We would spend hours upon hours cruising the streets of Gateway on our bikes. Living on the top of a court gave us a perfect place to ride endless circles. If you considered the court a clock, a little peddling from nine to twelve would earn you another effortless lap of coasting.

When the circling made us dizzy, we cruised down to Friendship Drive. This street had two distinct parts. If you took a left at the bottom of the hill, the street was perfectly flat and about eight yards long.

If you took a right at the bottom of the court, you headed down a steep slope that ended up on Janette Avenue and eventually the creek. There was a time for that right turn, but the breakneck speed down the hill had to be followed by pushing the bike back up.

By taking a left at the bottom of the court and another left at the end of Friendship Drive onto Marietta, you were headed towards "The Shady Place". Since most of our bike riding was done in the summer months when school was out of session, many of our rides were extremely hot. The Shady Place was a respite from the heat. Huge trees grew on both sides of the street, covering the entire area with shade, no matter the time of day or year. We spent numerous hours circling under the coverage of those cooling trees.

One routine summer day, we decided to race around the entire block. We started at our driveway on Friendship Court. The block consisted of a right turn on Friendship Drive, a right turn on Janette Avenue, a right turn on Kathy Avenue, a right turn on Marietta Avenue, a right turn on Friendship Drive, and a final right turn back onto Friendship Court.

We decided to take right turns so we didn't have to climb that steep, long hill at the end of the race. However, that meant climbing the not-as-steep, but three times as long, Kathy Avenue hill. Racing was always a ball but the outcome was never in question. It seemed someone always became exhausted and failed to finish. However, that was probably for the best. Making sharp turns at breakneck speed with the possibility of cars in your path wasn't the smartest thing to attempt.

As we grew older, we broadened the uses for our bikes. They became a mode of transportation and a tool to develop tricks. Riding a bike can grow very tiring to the body, especially the back. Even as a youngster, I remember how my back would ache. The best way to relieve the strain was to set straight up. However, sitting straight up made reaching the handle bars difficult it not impossible. There was a solution and we were bound and determined to figure out the trick of "no hands riding".

I hate to think of the awful spills I took learning to ride without hands. At the onset of this venture, we kept our hands just inches from the handle bars. At the first sign of unbalance, our hands reached for the safety of the bars. With practice, we were able to coast for ten to twenty feet without the need to use our hands.

The back relief mixed with pride and the

desire to push further caused us to continue to practice. Soon we were coasting hundreds of yards on straight-aways without the use of our hands. We sped down the court, made the right turn, and were able to coast, no-handed, all the way to the end of the street. The more comfortable we became without using our hands, the farther away they strayed from the handle bars. You would soon see us coasting down the street with our hands high above our heads, celebrating our own freedom and greatness.

We wanted something more and were determined to make it happen. The next step was peddling while not holding the handlebars. This proved to be a very difficult, dangerous task. Each time we pushed down with our feet, it threw off our balance. This was going to take a while to master. Self-confidence became the key. The more we allowed our hands to return to the bike, the easier it was to do the same the next time.

After many failed attempts, we began to see success, first a few feet, then several yards, and eventually the entire stretch of Friendship Drive. Peddling without hands was cool and we thought we were kings of the road.

We weren't satisfied with simply pedaling and coasting straight without using our hands. We decided to try to teach ourselves how to turn the bikes without using our hands. This actually came easier that the peddling stage. I think the fact that we learned to control and shift our weight leant itself to turning.

The key to turning a bike without hands was balance with a controlled shift and speed. You had to be going at least ten miles an hour to make it work. I learned to turn the bike to the right without hands but never the left. I think it must have had to do with my dominant hand.

The most unforgettable moment of no-hand riding came on a sunny day during the summer. Amy Campbell, possibly the most beautiful girl in the world at that time, was out playing in the court. She lived two houses to the right from us with her two sisters and parents.

Her father, Sonny, had an old, light blue pick-up truck that he always parked in the court. Amy was sitting on the back of the truck watching us ride. Doing what any young boy would do, I decided to showoff to catch her eye. What could be more impressive that riding down the court on my bike without hands, turning the corner, again without hands, and peddling down the street, again, without hands. So I took off and accomplished my feat, only to notice that she was seemingly unimpressed.

Trying to up the ante', I tried to think of something that would surely catch her eye. One thing came to mind; no-hands AND no-feet. I had never even attempted this but I felt Amy was worth an attempt.

I took off downhill, blinded by beauty and quickly ended up sprawled out on the concrete with every inch of my body in pain. Luckily, and remarkable, I didn't break any bones and the skin damage was minimal. The only good thing is I did get Amy's attention and she in turn got the attention of my parents to come scrape me off the asphalt.

We soon learned to pop wheelies on our bikes. Not only to pop them, but to get the front tire way up in the air and then peddle down the street, sort of like a unicycle with a spare. It was fun to use the curbs of the street to pop the wheelie, but by doing so we would wind up in a yard.

Though Ray was a pretty good ramp jumper, it never really caught on. I think too many times the board would break or the log would move and the jump would fail, so we left those antics to Evel Knievel.

The other use for our bikes was transportation. The creek was our most popular destination on our bikes. There were intermittent times when we rode our bikes to school, depending on grade, season, and weather. The coolest thing about being a bike rider to school was you got dismissed first, along with the bus riders. I believe this was to make sure the sidewalks were clear of potential ride-by victims.

We occasionally rode our bikes to Pleasant Green swimming pool. This was probably the best destination of all. We would arrive at the pool burning up from the trip and get to dive into the cool waters of the pool. On the return trip, our bathing suits and towels were soaked with water, keeping us cool for most of the journey. And once, Ray and I rode our bikes to Waldo's

Pizza in McHenry Center. That is a story within itself.

We rode up one summer lunchtime to eat pizza. We walked into the restaurant and decided what type of pizza we wanted to order. When the man behind the counter asked what size, Ray and I responded in unison, "Large".

The man began to chuckle and we grew slightly self-conscious, confused, and a little angry. He said to us, "If you boys can eat an entire large pizza, I'll buy you another one another day". We accepted the challenge and sat down to start in on that pizza.

Waldo's Pizza was the best around and the pizza that day was better than ever. As we ate, we discussed when we would be able to return to collect our free pizza. About half way through that pizza, we began to slow. I couldn't believe how full I was and how much pizza was still uneaten.

Ray and I agreed that there was no way there was going to be pizza left that day and continued to cram pizza into our already full bodies. After what seemed like hours, we finished the last piece. Somehow it didn't seem like a conquest.

We shuffled up to the cash register and showed the man the empty plate. He kept his promise and gave us a coupon for another free pizza. We returned to our bikes, only then realizing that we were in no condition to make the long trek back home.

I think we must have made fifty rest stops

between Waldo's and home. When we finally arrived at home, we made our way in to tell Mom and Dad of our great accomplishment and how we proved that fella wrong. When we rode to get our free pizza, we happily ordered a medium and had a much more enjoyable trip home that day.

Mike, circa, 1st Grade

Chapter 5
Fun Times

Christmas was always a special time in the Westveer household. Combining the eagerness of celebrating the birth of Christ with the anticipation of opening those wonderful wrapped boxes under the tree really exploded the excitement meter. I remember one Christmas morning in particular growing up. I was probably about ten years old at the time. Not only did I receive a really awesome bike that year but I was also introduced to the world of video gaming. I unwrapped a present that was called PONG. PONG was a video game system that hooked up to the television, allowing you to play games displayed on the screen.

This device had four game choices to play. The first was simply called Pong. Pong was where you played a tennis-like game, hitting the "ball" back and forth until someone missed it. You would maneuver your "paddle" by rotating a knob on the system. You could play against the computer or against a friend.

The second game was Double Pong, where a

second paddle was added to each side. This upped the difficulty of the game and was much faster paced. The third game was called Catch. Catch was the opposite of Pong. You had an opened space in a long line that you tried to let the ball go through.

The fourth and final game was a one person game in which you tried to maneuver the ball into a slot at the top of a wall on the opposite side. As you were successful, the slot became smaller and smaller.

I spent hours upon hours playing these games on a tiny black and white television set. I soon became very adept at playing and didn't find much competition in the household. Little did I know this was a very humble beginning to something that would continue to be a part of my life for a long time.

About the time we wore out the PONG game, I received another video gaming system; Odyssey, by Magnavox. This was a step up from the PONG game in many ways. The most obvious was that is was in color. The other major difference was that there were lots of games you could buy to be used with the system.

You had to purchase game cartridges to be placed into the game console. Sports games quickly became our favorite. Football was a big hit and we played for hours on end. You could see the whole field at once. It ran right to left on the television screen. Each team consisted of six players. On offense, you had three lineman, two receivers, and a quarterback.

The players looked like stick figures and were all one color, red or blue. To pass, you had to push the joystick towards the player and click the red button. This was a major upgrade from the turning of the knob on PONG to the joysticks of Odyssey.

Odyssey controllers were black. They consisted of a box about the size of a package of sliced cheese with a joy stick protruding from the center. The joystick could be pushed or pulled in eight directions, each noted by a groove. For any action that was to be done, there was a red button in the top right corner to be pushed. This device was plugged into the main Odyssey console.

Another favorite game was Baseball. This was way before the popularity of video games soared and games still had very simple names. baseball was Baseball and football was Football, and so on.

Baseball actually had nine players on each team, a breakthrough it seemed for sports gaming. Much like football, the teams were red and blue and looked like stick figures.

The infielders were stationary while the outfielders could move around. All three outfielders moved as one as you chased down batted balls.

The field was two dimensional and the outfield wall was a mere line. If a homerun was hit, it simply went through the wall. The baseball was a square.

My love for baseball stats was nourished by this game. I felt the need to keep track of how each player was doing (regardless of the fact that every player looked exactly alike and no names or numbers were included).

I copied real line-ups from the newspaper from the six teams I had chosen to place in my league. Of course, my beloved Cincinnati Reds were one of the chosen ones.

I hand drew a grid to keep box scores and Mom made copies for me at work. I spent hours playing games and keeping track of the scores and stats. I loved it then and I still love keeping baseball stats today.

The reason I had an Odyssey system was that Uncle Charlie had a contact in the Magnavox Company that gave my parents a great price. I remember the Christmas I received seven new games, a dream come true. I can still see the slick, new black boxes that the games came in. Very similar in size to today's VCR tapes, you would flip open the front cover to reveal the game. I kept all the games in an old, green, wooden cart.

An add-on product soon came out that took video game technology to a new level. Until the release of this new innovation, there was not any sound with the system. This new device, *The*

Voice, added sound. It was half the size of the main console and pushed in to the console as if a game. You then pushed the game into *The Voice*.

This was great, but only games made specifically for this device benefited. We bought the Pac-Man type game and were thrilled to hear things like "watch out" or "great job" being shouted at us through the new device as we played the game.

The Lewis family later got an Intellivision system that had better graphics and sound. The Odyssey began having to share time with the Lewis system. Since those early years, our family has seen many systems come and go: Atari, Nintendo, Super Nintendo, Sega, PlayStation, PlayStation II, Game Cube, Xbox, Wii, PlayStation III and countless other handheld and plug in systems and devices. You can only imagine what the future holds.

When video games became boring or our parents wanted to watch television, the board games came off the shelves. I can not count the times that Monopoly was put into play and never finished. Other favorites were Checkers, Connect Four, Clue, and Risk.

The game I remember playing the most was a biblical trivia game that the Lewis' owned. We played it every time their Uncle Mark would come over. Mark was not much older than us, even though he carried the uncle title.

Their mother's youngest sibling was stricken with Muscular Dystrophy. He would come over in his wheelchair and we would set up the game on the outside picnic table. We would play for hours and Mark would have a ball. Mark lived much longer than the doctor's said he would and I cherished getting to know him.

There were lots of things to entertain us in and around the neighborhood. Two houses to the left, the "Old Lady's House", had a short, but steep hill. We enjoyed taking large, cut up boxes and sliding down the hill. If we didn't have cardboard, we just rolled down the hill, ending up in a pile at the bottom with the world spinning.

Flying kites was a beloved activity on warm, windy days. Living in a subdivision with closely built homes meant lots of wiring ran above our heads. Utility poles held electrical, phone, and later cable wiring. Finding an appropriate place to fly a kite and not end up tangled in a knotty mess was a chore. Through trial and error, we settled on our next door neighbor's backyard. The Barnes had a big back yard clear of trees and wires that was the perfect setting for kite flying.

One invention we came up with to further the fun was tying the kite to fishing string attached to a rod and reel. Once the kite got up into the wind stream, it appeared you had hooked a large fish, maybe an Angel Fish. I remember chasing a detached kite all the way to Gateway School through many yards and over many fences, as it slowly settled back to Earth.

Another thing that provided entertainment for us during dull times involved vehicles and fruit.

At the far end of our backyard was a shabby looking tree. Once a year it would produce huge fruit. These cabbage sized things were light green with wrinkled coverings. Not really knowing what to call these green balls, we referred to them as mock oranges or crab apples.

The word on the street was that these green giants were poisonous. True or false, we chose not to tempt fate, making sure our hands never got close to our mouths. We gathered up as many "oranges" as we could carry and headed towards Kathy Avenue.

We placed the mock oranges in the middle of the road, evenly spaced to create maximum coverage. The idea was to get cars to run over them, smashing them into oblivion. After we had them like we wanted, we hid so that we could see the road but the driver's wouldn't see us. It was fun to watch (and hear) cars crushing the mock oranges. Occasionally, one would be barely nipped and sent rolling or drivers would maneuver around the obstacles, but sooner all later all the oranges were demolished.

Tree climbing was also a popular past time. There were several trees we climbed, including the one that had grown into the fence behind the Shelton's house, or the two in front of the West's house on Friendship Drive. But the tree that was climbed most often and yielded the most fun was the one in the Campbell's backyard.

    Mr. Sonny Campbell, Amy's daddy, had made a rope swing that hung from high up in this tree. We always climbed up from the back with help from a tire that leaned against the tree. We would reach up and grab the branch right above us, using this leverage to shimmy around to the main branch to the right. Once on the main branch we scooted over to the launching spot.

    This branch was rubbed smooth from years of children scooting across its bark. Right in the center of this branch was a dip just large enough to sit in, much like a swing set seat. Somebody on the ground would push the rope swing up and the limb sitter would attempt a catch. It often took several attempts to get the swing up to the swinger.

    When the rope was caught, it was time to take to the air. The climber turned swinger would slide off the end of the branch and begin the swing. Back and forth we would go, each trip just a little lower and slower.

    We would sometimes go off in pairs, try swinging off in different positions, or regrabbing the branch on our first backswing. That amazing branch could hold about four people.

    I do not remember a time growing up when I did not have a dog. At an age too early for me to remember, we had a Chihuahua named Cricket. The first dog I actually remember was Bruno.

Bruno was a Dachshund, lovingly called a wiener dog. He was brownish red and small, even for a Dachshund. Bruno was very sweet and loved to just lay on the floor and have his belly rubbed. He could also sit up for minutes while begging for scraps of food at the table.

I recall coming out of the house one school morning and sitting on the front porch, trying to peel a record piece of paint of the concrete. Mom joined me and said that Bruno had died. Daddy had accidentally run over Bruno as he left for work. Bruno had a bad habit of chasing him down the court as he drove to work each morning. This particular morning, he caught the car.

The next dog we owned was Barney, another Dachshund dog. He didn't have as much red as Bruno, but was another sweet dog. He too could sit up for scraps with the best of them.

Unfortunately, he met with the same fate as Bruno. When I got home from school one day, I noticed Daddy digging in the far corner of the back yard. I questioned Mom about what Daddy was doing. It was then I learned that Barney had been run over by a car.

Our next dog was a Cocker Spaniel by the name of Brandee. Brandee learned one of the neatest tricks I had ever seen a dog perform. She lived parts of her day in a cage in the den. She learned to not only push the cage open to exit the cage, but also to grab the cage with her claws and pull it open. All we had to do was say "Cage" and she would pull the door open and go into the cage.

Brandee lived a full life, making the move with us to the other side of the city. She was the first of three Cocker Spaniels our family owned. Sisters Sadie and Slugger joined our families in later years.

We tried to make several other animals into pets that weren't meant to be pets. Catching lightning bugs, or fire flies, was something we enjoyed throughout our childhood summers. Occasionally we decided to put a lot of the bugs into a jar and take it into the house. It made a really neat night light for a while.

The problem was that even with ventilating the top of the jar, there was only so much oxygen to be breathed by our captors. Rarely did the lightning bugs last through one night. It was easy to tell what had occurred because the smell was horrendous the following morning.

Box turtles were known to make an occasional appearance in our house, but failed to last long due to boredom. Turtles didn't like to be petted, they wouldn't run around and play with you, and they didn't seem to appreciate being stared at and observed. That combination didn't make for much of a pet.

Fish and fish tanks came and went as the years passed. I used to love to set the tank up and get a school of Neon Tetras. These fish glowed red and light blue and seemed to love to show off their colors.

Other fish we had were Angel Fish, Cardinal Tetras, Tiger Barbs, Guppies, Algae Eaters, and Silver Dollars. Apparently our love of the fish didn't match up with the required work it took to maintain them. The tank would gradually get dirtier and the algae would cover the sides.

By the time an emergency cleaning would occur, many or most of the fish would be lost. The cycle would be to clean out the tank enough to be stored, and then the next time the fish whim came along, we would dig out the tank and the supplies and give it another shot. I'm not sure this was what was meant by the circle of life.

The most amazing animal story I recall from Gateway involved a wild rabbit. We were riding bikes on Friendship Drive while a group of older boys were playing football. Like most days, neighborhood dogs were running around as we played. Everything seemed to be normal until the dogs went wild and gathered near the side of a house.

Curious to see what the disturbance was, we jumped off our bikes and went towards the dogs. Somehow emerging from the pack was a rabbit.

This rabbit looked darker than most rabbits and seemed to be dragging something. Only when we got closer did we understand what was happening. The dogs had actually skinned the rabbit alive. This rabbit was running around without fur. We quickly shooed the dogs away and took a closer look at the animal.

It was odd. There was no blood and the rabbit

looked fine. Little did we know the rabbit was in deep shock and would only last a small amount of time. One of the older boys took the rabbit away. It made us look at our dogs differently. How could our loving pets turn into rabbit killers and then act as if nothing happened?

An intriguing discovery we made while roaming the neighborhood was caterpillars. Huge white webs looming in the trees caught our attention. It was much too large for a spider and like nothing we had seen before. Swarming inside and around this "web" and on the branches close by were caterpillars. They were black and yellow with beady eyes. They had furry coats and stood up if you touch their backs.

These furry little creatures caught our eyes. We started taking a few back home to watch closer. I took some home and put them in a container. I added leaves and sticks and placed the container in my bedroom. The little fellow seemed to thrive, but the odor was horrible. I'm not sure if it was the rotting plants or the caterpillar itself, but it had to go.

As we messed around the web, or as we later found out, the community cocoon, we found that inside its walls were hundreds of the creatures. We begin to break holes in their canopy and snatch the creatures from their homes and put them in the famous bucket. We hurried back home to try out a fascinating idea.

Caterpillar races were about to begin. We sat up two by fours to make a race track and then dumped the critters out. Apparently, this was going to take a while. Half of the worms landed on their backs and struggled just to get on its feet. Others headed back in the bucket and many others headed in the totally wrong directions. We quickly surmised that the ones heading the correct way were the only ones with any promise and quickly separated them from the clueless critters.

After collecting all the caterpillars with potential, we got ready to start the race. A funny thing happened. We had the same things happen again, back rollers, wrong wayers, strayers, and racers, only this time in smaller numbers.

We decided we would focus on just a few of the critters that seem to have the most promise. We each chose one caterpillar, named that sucker, and placed it at the starting line. When we released them, it did have some semblance of a race.

I'm not sure what the appeal of the caterpillars and their homes was, but we made it our mission to catch every caterpillar who dared build a home near ours. We never were able to watch one mature to a butterfly. I guess we had the same luck with butterflies as we did with tadpoles.

Mike and Ray celebrating their father Newel's birthday.

    There was once a time in Nashville history when it really snowed. Not the highly anticipated flurries that the local weathermen tease us with, but real snow measured in inches, not flakes.

    Once Bill Hall, famous local weatherman, pulled the Davidson County piece off the map to reveal that beautiful snow that told us we were out of school for the day, we began preparations. Forget sleeping in, we were ready for a day of freezing fun. The options were limitless, but sledding was probably the most popular snow day activity.

Ray and I had Western Flyer sleds. These were the real deal. Real wood slats combined with strong steel runners provided the ultimate sledding machine. To top it off, a cross bar near the front of the sled provided steering. These gems had everything a sledder needed except for brakes. To stop we used our feet or just the nearest tree.

The best sledding spot was found on Kathy Avenue. Just up from the Lewis home, in front of the Shelton's home, was the starting point. From there we had approximately a quarter mile ride before coasting to a stop near Janette Avenue.

The Lewis boys had nice wooden sleds too and we would put on the winter gear and head towards the Gateway slopes. The gear consisted of whatever we needed to put on to stay warm and hopefully dry. The oddest item we adorned were plastic bags. We put these bags on our feet, over our socks and under our boots. This was to protect us from frostbite that could occur with extended exposure to the cold.

We would spend extended hours exposed not only to the weather but to tons of wintry fun. Gloves, multiple pairs of socks, a couple of coats, and a stocking cap that covered your face rounded out the winter wardrobe.

We looked like a group of penguins waddling

out into the snow with all the layers of clothing we were wearing. We grabbed our sleds out of the shed, threw them over the fence into the Lewis yard, and carried them to the launching pad on Kathy Avenue.

A running start was a must for a good sled ride. Depending on the conditions, this in and of itself, could be a chore. You would hold the sled in front of you with both hands, take off running and when you reached maximum speed, or just tuckered out, jumped aboard the sled for the downhill trip.

If the snow was deep, the sledding would be slow. Cutting those initial tracks into the newly fallen blanket of snow was wonderful, but also sluggish. As trip after trip was taken down the hill, the snow became packed down and the sledding speeds picked up. If the day was cloudy and the temperature stayed cold, the speeds increase even more.

Our sledding "course" was very simple. The initial part of the route was straight and the steepest. It ran past the Hunt, Lewis, and Hunley houses. Then there was a very slight turn to the left. This part is where the hill lessened but speed was pretty much maintained. The third and final part of the trip was where the hill almost flattened and speed slowly decreased until you came to a stop. Depending on the conditions, you could almost make it to the end of the street.

The old saying of "What goes up must come

down" would be reversed on sled days. After sledding down the hill, you faced a trip back up, dragging the sled behind. We would often work out deals to share in the hauling by hooking sleds together and one person carrying more than one sled. After each trip down, the hike back up became more difficult as fatigue set in. The best way up was usually in front yards instead of the street. The footing was better and if you did take a fall, the landing was just a little softer.

We continually looked for ways to make the sledding more adventurous. One of the adaptations that was made was in the way we rode the sled. The best (in my opinion) and most used way was lying on the sled on your stomach, facing downhill, and steering with your hands. This was the method that allowed for a running start and also provided the best steering.

An alternate way to sled was by sitting on the sled. This was a much slower ride because you couldn't have a running start to build up momentum. With this style, you would be sitting on your bottom with your feet pointed towards the front. You used your feet to steer the sled. This was the best way to go down with a friend on the same sled.

In Olympic years, we decided we were going to luge like we saw on television. This entailed laying on your back, feet forwards to steer, and raising your head just enough to see. While not the best for street sledding, it made us appreciate those guys we saw going full steam ahead for the gold.

There were other attempts made to make it down the hill, such as standing, being on our knees, laying on our backs-heads first, crossed-legged, etc., but most met with disaster and we eventually stayed with the common positions.

Besides changing the way we rode the sled, we experimented with having more than one rider per sled. The most common attempt would be for one rider to get a running start while the second rider would jump aboard further down the hill. This proved to be a balancing act which resulted in many spills occurring at the beginning of the descent.

Quite often, the second rider would knock the first rider off when jumping on or the second rider would leap right over the sled, to end up sprawled sledless in the road. We did eventually master this technique and the added weight made the sleds go faster. The bottom rider was the steerer and needed to be at least as large on the top rider in order not to be smashed.

Although being sandwiched between wooden sled slats and a friend while going full speed down a slick street was thrilling, it could also be painful. After the initial "umph" of boarding and the subsequent boarding of kid number two, knees and elbows often found themselves pushing down into the driver, causing pain, and for the top passenger, often an early exit.

The advantage of being on the bottom and driving is that you could decide to deboard the person on top of you. All it took was a sudden turn of the sled and a shift of the body and off they went. Of course, this was great fun for both people involved. Body surfing would be a good description of what would happen to the ejected fellow.

The momentum that had been built continued whether you were aboard a sled or not. The thrown person continued sliding down the ice, leaving a body path instead of the normal two runner lines. The major obstacle became dodging other sledders who were making their way down the hill. Evading people who decide you make a good target was not easy.

Once the riders caught onto the game of "buck off the passenger", things got interesting. Riders tended to hold on a little tighter and fight to stay on a little harder. It became a contest to see who would be on the sled, if anyone, when it came to a stop. If both boys ended up off the sled, the victory went to the rider. Not only did the driver lose, they had to chase the sled that continued on its path regardless of being manned.

The ultimate accomplishment was to be the top rider, somehow manage to disembark the driver, and take control of the sled. The remainder of the ride would be celebrated as if a world championship was just claimed. The shamed, dethroned driver could only hang his head in embarrassment and start the trek back up the hill.

Another thing we loved to do while sledding

was form chains. We would grab the runners of the person sledding in front of you. The fun part of doing this was the snakelike motion you could create by steering back and forth. The back person would follow the path of the person in front, eventually. If you made a sharp enough turn, you could actually see the person a few sleds behind you.

As we became more skilled and creative, we started sharing the lead on the way down. The person in front would be released, steer off to the side a little ways, dig his toes into the snow to slow down, wait for the train to pass, and then grab hold of the last rider. It was a contest to see if we could go all the way through the line and have the starting driver be at the front when we got to the bottom of the hill.

We also enjoyed whipping each other as we sled. Not in the spanking mode, but grabbing someone else's sled and either yanking really hard to send you forward, or by grabbing their runners and propelling them faster down the hill.

As true in everything we did, competition was a must, and sled racing was a big deal. We would line up across the street, on our sleds, ready to race. We seldom raced from a running start, preferring instead to start from the lying forward position. When the starter would yell go, we would "paddle" with all our might to build up momentum.

There were two main types of races, hands-on and hands-off. The hands-off races were pure racing. You would not interfere with other racers in anyway.

Winning the race would result from your push start, the path you chose down the hill, and the condition of your runners. Racers looked for icy spots going down the hill. They were faster than riding through the snow.

Steering was very important. The straighter line you could follow to the bottom, the better. Any turn, no matter how small, would slow down your sled. Decisions would have to be made if a quick turn to reach an icy spot was worth the temporary decrease in speed.

Being in the lead early was a big advantage. The runners would send up icy streams of slush to hinder the sight of the sledders who followed. It also kept you out of the bumping and grinding that normally came with a close race. The better racers would keep an eye out for the competitors to see who was gaining and what route they took. It was common for the leader to block any advances that were made by the competition, or to stop any drafting that might be occurring, NASCAR style.

The second classification of racing was "full-contact". This was by far the more popular and the most played out going down Kathy Avenue. Beginning at the starting line, and often long before, any and everything that could be done to gain an advantage was done or at least attempted.

Whether it was yanking the sled in front of you to propel yourself forward while pulling them backward or trying to pull or push an opponent off their sled, everything was fair game. Forcing another sled off the road was frequently attempted and occasionally accomplished.

When we were having double passenger races, the top rider became a valuable asset. Whether it was launching himself off his sled to take out another or being the lookout for oncoming threats, he was just as valuable as the steerer.

Snowfalls, especially deep wet ones, seemed to bring out an interest in construction. What could we make out of this snow? How could we move it around to our advantage?

Making snowballs was the obvious answer. Not just the size to throw at someone, but snowballs bigger than us. Snow boulders might have been a better name. By forming a ball about the size of a person's head and then rolling it through the wet, clinging snow, you could very quickly create a monster, an massive snowball.

We usually started at the top of our backyard and pushed the ball downhill towards the far corner. If we had enough people, we would attempt to push it back up again. These giant creations were extremely heavy and became unmovable at a certain size.

One hazard we encountered was getting the ball moving downhill so fast we couldn't stop it.

Luckily our backyard was enclosed and our neighbors were not at risk of getting clobbered by a runaway snowball.

Of course, this too became a competition. Who could build the biggest ball? Who could push their ball up the hill the fastest? However, we did team up and help each other to create countless giant balls.

The question became, "What can we do with these giant snowballs?" The answer to that question was to create huge forts to be used during snowball fights. We would build as many giant snowballs as possible and simply push them all together to form a barrier, or fort.

The forts evolved through trial and error like many of our escapades. Questions such as where to locate the forts arose. There appeared to be two answers to that question. If we wanted to "fight" each other, almost anywhere would work; as long as the two forts were close enough to be reached by a thrown snowball. If we wanted to ambush our parents or unexpecting traffic, location was much more important.

The building of the fort itself became the primary source of fun. We worked feverously to turn giant balls of snow into something that loosely resembled a fort. Much like the building of sand castles, we carved sections off and built up sections in other places. When the snowfall reached six or more inches, we had enough 'building supplies' to go all out.

We quickly discovered that bigger was not always better. If the walls of the forts were over our heads, we couldn't see the approaching enemy and were easy pickings' for a surprise attack.

We decided the best size snowballs for making the initial wall, or barrier, was about three feet high. This was high enough to protect us from hard thrown balls from the enemy, but low enough to launch a counter attack. By sitting down with your back against the snow wall or by being on your knees, you were safe from everything except the most perfectly placed lob.

The urge became to build ever increasingly more elaborate structures. One of the first changes we made had to do with the giant snowballs themselves. We discovered that if we split the snowballs in half top to bottom, we would instantly double our wall space. The rational was that half of the ball was still about two feet thick and would provide ample strength to stop even the best thrown snowballs.

It also created flat walls on the inside of the fort. This allowed much more safety than the previous round ones. You could push yourself flat against the snow, cutting down the angle to an almost impossible feat for the enemy. Of course the problem with splitting snowballs was that often they crumble while we were trying to split them, leaving a heap of unformed snow.

Another alteration we made was to create a place to store snowballs. We decided to dig into one of the constructed walls and create a place to stash our premade snowballs. We also decided to fill in the gaps between snowballs. We did so by packing snow into the gaps to create a solid wall.

Though the main purpose of our fort was to bomb each other with snowballs it became more like an outside clubhouse. We decided that we needed furniture and built small ice blocks or snow blocks to sit on. We also built interior walls to create separate rooms for each person.

When boredom set in from lack of an attack we became even more creative with our building. I remember digging holes through the bottom of the structure to create tunnels in and out of the fort. It was truly amazing to see what idle hands could create.

One year we had a 6 in. snowfall followed closely by extremely cold temperatures. This created the very crunchy type of snow that was useless in building snowballs, snowman, or a snow fort. In fact it was frozen so hard you could almost walk across the snow without leaving footprints. We decided to try something new. We took the snow shovel and cut blocks out of the snow.

Cutting blocks was very easy but the difficulty came when we tried to pick up the blocks. The snow closer to the ground was not frozen as stiff and tended to fall apart when we picked it up. We made a quick adjustment and decided only to cut 4 inches deep into the snow to get our blocks.

This worked perfectly and we were on our way to building our igloo.

Wanting to emulate my father the architect, I took the lead and designed our fledgling structure. It was extremely important that all the blocks were cut to the same dimensions. This would ensure that our igloo would stand straight and remain strong.

It became quickly evident that not all of the construction team appreciated my desire for precision and standards. Freestyle seemed to be the prevailing thought as our igloo took shape. What shape it became was up for discussion. Needless to say, I was unappreciative of the effort and felt vindicated when it soon fell to the ground.

I took it upon myself to independently construct my own igloo. I meticulously cut the snow blocks from the hardened snow using the snow shovel, being careful to consider the curvature of the shovel. I made the decision to make my igloo perfectly square.

I scraped an area clean and started the long, steady building process. Using the width of the shovel, the blocks were cut into about eighteen inch squares. After several failed attempts to move this size of bock, I started cutting the blocks in half. This worked perfectly and the building began to take shape.

Each side was approximately four feet in length. I decided that there would be one entrance and a small window. The walls grew to two feet in height on all sides when three things converged. The sun was going down quickly, the available snow was running low, and I was whooped.

I decided to leave the building until the morning and called it a day. I went into the house to thaw out and plan the strategy for completing the igloo. During the evening I took several peeks out of the window to admire my work (and pray it was still standing).

The next morning I was thrilled to find that not only was my igloo still standing, it was improved. An amazing thing happened while I slept. The temperature dipped to near zero, further hardening each brick. It was now one hardened piece of ice and envied by those who deserted the effort the previous day.

I considered how I could complete my igloo. With very little available snow to add to the structure, I decided this would have to do in height and width. A large piece of plywood that Daddy had stored in the out-building fit perfectly atop the igloo and became the improvised roof.

I threw some snow on top of the wood roof to try to conceal the shortcut in construction and add to its beauty. Sliding in on my belly, I entered into the world of the Inuit.

I could barely move but thoroughly enjoyed my success. This solo project would slowly melt away, but the satisfaction of a job well-done would stay with me for a long time.

Snow is one of those magic things that seem to excite the kid in all of us. Little did I know as a grade school student that the teachers and principal were more excited about snow and the possibility of a snow day than the students. However, I remember one particular snow that became a worrisome situation.

Daddy worked in downtown Nashville at the Baptist Sunday School Board. Snow started falling during the day and schools and businesses began closing early. We were all home except for Daddy. We were involved in playing in the snow and didn't have a worry. However, as it got later and later and Daddy still hadn't arrived home, we began to stir nervously.

I remember sitting in front of the living room windows waiting for the white Monte Carlo to turn onto the court. The sun had gone down and the snow continued to pile up. Every time lights appeared we became excited that Daddy had made it home safe, only to be disappointed when it was another neighbor. After what seemed like days and bed time neared, the beautiful sight of Daddy driving up the court was in the window. Even as a child, I remember how calm Daddy was and wondered how he remained that way. We never rationed hugs and kisses in our family, but I'm guessing Daddy received a record number that night when he walked through the door.

Mike, his brother Ray and their mother, Joanne.

Like many of the boys of my generation, I collected baseball cards. There were few things more exciting than slowly flipping through a pack of fresh baseball cards, coated with a dusting of bubble gum powder. When I started collecting cards, there was only one brand, Topps. Every year we anticipated what that year's version would look like. You could always count on specific information being included on the front; name, team, and position. The difference would be in the layout, style and specialty cards.

I put great thought into which individual pack of cards to buy each time I had to chance to make a purchase. Which pack contained that year's superstar or rookie? My favorite pack to buy was the triple packs that could be found at McCrory's in Rivergate Mall. You could see six cards before you bought a pack. Sealed in plastic in three small piles, you could look at the front of three cards and the backs of three more. Sometimes I spent the entire time we were at the mall searching for the perfect pack.

The backs of baseball cards were chucked full of information. We studied the year by year statistics of every player. Records and career highs were written in italics. Also included on the backs were interesting facts about players. Long before cards became high priced commodities, we thought of them as toys.

We made up games to play with the cards. The most common was simulating a game. We picked our teams from the available cards and decide on our line-ups. On the den carpet, the home team would position his players into their defensive positions. The visitors placed their lead-off hitter up to bat. Using a paper wad, the pitcher would flip the wad towards the batter. The batter would then try to hit the flipped wad by swatting at it with the baseball card. We were oblivious to the damage we were doing to possibly valuable cards.

In the late 1980s, two additional baseball companies emerged, Donruss and Fleer. I gobbled up as many packs as I could afford, intrigued by their debut. The cards were very inferior in quality to the Topps cards, but we still couldn't get enough. Mistakes began to be found in the new cards and interest peaked in the card collecting community. Error cards, as they were known, began to have huge value. This was the first time we thought of the cards as anything but fun. I never understood why a backwards P on a Pittsburgh Pirates hat or a misspelled name would make a card more valuable. It went against what I always knew as true, mistakes are bad.

    I also started collecting bottle lids. I'm not sure how, or why, this hobby started, but I soon had a budding collection of useless, smelly, and slightly bent from opening, bottle caps. Whenever walking, I found myself looking down at the ground for additions to my collection. This corny collection soon paid big dividends. While searching for caps at Elm Hill Park one day while waiting for Adrian Lewis' softball practice to end, I made a nice discovery.

    In a parking lot, under a car, was a man's diamond ring. At first, I thought it was fake, but soon found out it was real. We waited to make sure none of the players had lost the ring. When the parking lot emptied and no one made a claim, Adrian said it was mine. Far from having fingers large enough to wear the ring, I gave it to my father. He wore the ring proudly for many years.

    The final collection I compiled as a child was my Sports Illustrated cover collection. This collection doubled as room décor. Every week when I received my copy of the magazine in the mail, I tore off the cover and pinned it to my bedroom wall. It was really neat seeing all of that era's stars compiled into a collage above my bed. Of course the swimsuit issue always received preferential placement.

Family portrait, courtesy of Sears!

Chapter 6
Holidays

Our family loved to celebrate holidays throughout the year. Mom and Dad made sure we received gifts, dressed up, ate well, or whatever each holiday called for traditionally. I have interwoven many of those childhood traditions into my own children's celebrations.

Halloween was not nearly as commercial, or controversial, as it is currently. It was simply a fun time of year. Costumes came in simple boxes and consisted of a plastic apron like pullover and a facemask held on by a rubber band.

We changed into our costumes and anxiously awaited our parents to say it was time to go. We went door to door trick-or-treating, hoping for that favorite piece of candy at each home. Gateway subdivision was a perfect setting for a windfall of treat. The houses were close together, most families knew each other, and the streets were well lit.

After returning home from our night out, we would dump the contents of our bags onto the living room carpet. This served two purposes; to see what our haul contained and to let our parent's inspect the candy. This was necessary to make sure some lunatic didn't give us something that could harm us. One of Mom's favorite things to do was to eat a piece of candy and say, "I need to check this for poison".

Once the all clear was given we dove into the treats. We ate like somebody was lurking nearby to take our candy. We also worked deals with each other to get more of our favorites.

Today in late October, it seems like every church, school, and city has an event. Fall Festivals, Autumn Harvests, Trunk or Treat, and thousands of other events happen in lieu of traditional trick-or-treating. The first event of that manner that I remember was held at Rivergate Mall.

Each store in the mall was giving out candy as part of a promotional stunt. As part of my costume, I wore a pull-over mask of an old man. As we went from store to store, somewhere along the way, I pulled off my mask to cool down. I must have put it down and failed to realize it was missing until we saw the same mask on a manikin in a men's clothes store. Unable to prove it was mine, I left Rivergate Mall without my mask. A bag full of candy helped lessen the disappointment.

Easter was a fun time at the Westveer household. We awoke to find the Easter Bunny had visited during the night and left Ray and I baskets. There was usually a stuffed animal and lots of candy sitting atop the fake grass.

We started the day by dressing in our Sunday's finest and headed off to church. Following church we would have a great Easter dinner. After lunch we dyed, hunted, and ate boiled eggs throughout the remainder of the day.

One of my favorite memories of Easter happened in Kingston, Tennessee, at the home of my grandparents, Paul and Susie King. Most of my sixteen cousins, Ray, and I were going to have an Easter egg hunt in their backyard. The uncles and aunts hid the eggs and we were unleashed to hunt them down.

Besides Davi, I was the youngest of all the cousins. While the bigger kids raced around gathering eggs from their hiding places, I occasionally picked up the obvious, barely hidden ones and put them in my basket. All the eggs were quickly found, except for one, the Golden Egg.

The Golden Egg was the prize egg that usually contained money. It remained unclaimed and Uncle Charlie was enjoying the moment. He was playing the old warmer-colder game. I was listening closely and when he said I was hot, I noticed a bulge in his sock. I found the Golden Egg. Uncle Charlie had hidden the egg on himself.

Christmas has always been my favorite holiday. I couldn't wait for the lights, the music, the gifts, the decorations, and especially the birth of Jesus. Our family has always celebrated

Christmas in a big way. Ray and I have carried on a lot of these traditions with our own children.

The day after Thanksgiving was the day we usually set up the Christmas tree. We hauled the artificial tree from under the house and placed it in the living room. This spot was chosen because of the double-wide window that allowed for the tree's lights to be seen from the court.

Our family Christmas tree was iconic. It was the only tree I ever knew as a child. Putting it up was a big deal and much like working a puzzle. Each level of the tree was color coded by painted stems. The order of colors was written on the "trunk" of the tree. We would copy down the colors in order, put the two pieces of the trunk together, and we were ready to start.

Dad was meticulous in organizing things and was on the top of his game in storing and unpacking the tree. Each color, or group, of stems was bundled together and taped with duct tape. We would start with the largest stems and work our way up. Each individual stem had to be sculpted to look like part of the tree. You did this by bending the wire and spreading out the "pine needles".

As we neared the top, the games began. Who would get to place the topper branch? This was the "headpiece" of the tree. It usually ended up being Ray simply because I couldn't reach the top of the tree.

Now it was time to place the decorations. We used colored lights on the tree, sometimes blinking, other times not. Some years we would use garland, other years icicles or flocking. The number of ornaments grew every year as we added to our family collection. Ray and I made many of the ornaments we placed on the tree.

The highlight was placing the angel on top of the tree. We tried to alternate years between Ray and me but it was hard to remember. One year I remember returning after we had decorated the tree, taking the angel off, and then returning her to her perch just so I could say I put it on.

Christmas Eve was when the excitement really took hold. We would attend the Christmas Eve service at our church, First Baptist Church of Goodlettsville. The singing, lighting of the candles, and telling the Christmas story was always a joy and put us in the Christmas mood for all the right reasons. After the service, we would spend the rest of the evening with the Mullinaxs.

Whether at their house or ours, we had a great time. Sausage balls, trail mix, chess squares, hot chocolate, and a table full of other treats were devoured.

I would soon beg to go to bed to make the morning come as quick as possible, knowing even if I was in the bed, sleep would be hard to achieve. We said our good nights to the Mullinaxs and called it an evening. Once in bed, I dreamed of what the morning would bring. Walking down that hall and peeking around the corner to see all of those wonderful gifts was pure magic.

One of our family traditions that I have reluctantly become a part of was losing gifts. It never failed that Mom would hide some of our gifts around the house only to forget where she put them. It wasn't uncommon to get that last gift sometime in February. I remember stumbling across a misplaced gift one day in the laundry room. I was scavenging for Coke bottles to return to Kroger for the nickel rebate when I came across a forgotten gift. It was a simple, but addictive hand held toy that would have been quickly tossed aside on Christmas morning, but now kept me entertained for hours.

One Christmas season I decided I would take an early peek at some of my gifts. One day while I was alone in the house, I carefully partly unwrapped one of my gifts. It was a Tampa Bay Buccaneers long sleeve shirt. I remember the guilt almost ruining that Christmas for me. Never again have I even attempted to find out what someone was gifting to me. In fact, I take extra precautions to make sure ever gift I receive is truly a surprise.

Valentine's Day, Fourth of July, Thanksgiving, and all the other holidays, major and minor, were celebrated in our family. We've got to be careful not to overlook the true meaning of our Christian holidays, but making memories and building traditions will continue to be a part of the Westveer family.

Chapter 7
Church

From our birth, Ray and I were taken to church. My first stop as a newborn was Alta Loma Baptist Church, located extremely close to Gateway subdivision. However, due to unsafe wiring in the nursery, my family moved their membership to First Baptist Church Goodlettsville, were I attended until I moved off to college, and where I later got married.

Some of my earliest memories of church are of Sunday School. I remember playing with wooden blocks Sunday after Sunday. There were all shapes and sizes to build the greatest of buildings. I remember how loud they would be when they crashed to the ground. They were later replaced with the quieter cardboard style.

I also remember doing puzzles. The one that always seemed to show up was of a little girl. She looked Asian and had on a little dress. I was amused to see that same puzzle some thirty years later in my youngest son's Sunday School Class.

I also remember the Sunday School music. We marched to the song *I'm in the Lord's Army* and did the movements to *Do Your Ears Hang Low* over and over. We would bang on the tambourine and clap our hands as we marched in a never ending circle.

I don't recall this next story, but Mom says it is the truth. Apparently Julie Moore and I were kissing in the corner of Sunday School at the age of two. Julie and I were friends throughout the years and ended up graduating from Goodlettsville High School together.

Royal Ambassadors, or R.A.s, was the Wednesday night group for school aged boys that followed Children's Choir. We would study about missionaries and do really neat projects. Often being the only boy in children's choir, it was nice to be surrounded with guys. We would usually have some sort of lesson on a missionary and then head outside for kickball.

One Wednesday, Donnie Smith and I got into an argument during Royal Ambassadors. I can't recall what the fuss was about, but I'm sure it was important to world security. It had been raining for the entire day and the R.A. counselor preferred to keep us in that Wednesday night. However, we convinced him to allow us to go outside. Donnie and I began fussing and the next thing I remember, we were fighting.

It didn't take long for Donnie to get the advantage. He quickly was a top of me and had my face in the mud. Luckily, the teachers came to my rescue, separated us, and got our parents. Donnie and I remained friends for years and I am thankful for him proving to me at an early age that fighting was not in my best interest. It was the only time I was involved in a fight, so my record stands at 0-1, the loss coming by TKO.

I had a friend at church by the name of Molly Garrett. Sometime in the early elementary grades, she was diagnosed with leukemia. This was the first time I had to deal with a life threatening illness close to home. I remember sitting in sixth grade Sunday School, in a large circle with Molly. She had a bandana around her head, hiding the fact that she had lost her hair from chemotherapy. This was the last time I saw Molly. She passed away a short time later. I remember sitting at the table and Mom sharing the sad news about Molly's death.

One of the things that irritated me most about church actually had nothing to do with church. I loved to leave church in the fall and go home and watch NFL football. My family didn't share that love with me and instead favored going out to eat. Whether it was Shoney's or Rax, I knew I was in for a long meal.

Just about this time, salad bars were coming into existence. Mom, Dad and Ray loved salad bars. I tried my hand at making salads, too. My salads would consist of lots of croutons, sunflower seeds, bacon bits, pepperoni slices, and diced ham covered with Thousand Island dressing. They used to make fun of my concoction and Ray still calls it a Mike Style Salad.

I would quickly finish my Rax Roast Beef Sandwich or Shoney's Slim Jim and be ready to go, eager to watch the day's games. The rest of the family was enjoying their salads to the hilt and in no hurry to go anywhere. When it appeared they were finished, I was repeatedly horrified when they returned to the salad bar, over and over. I think it was a game to see who could make the most trips. Even though I loved the restaurant Rax, when it went under, I felt I had the last laugh.

Our church was a landmark in the community. It was often referred to as the spaceship church because of the prominent steeple that rose high into the sky. The white-washed concrete structure made a beautiful, inspiring sight against a clear blue sky.

Sitting next to the church was a house owned by the church that was occasionally used for gatherings. The house didn't have an official name and was hard to describe when referring to it. The pastor, Brother Abbington, held a contest to give the house an official name. There were two winners, Mrs. Abbington and me. The winning name - The House. The creative idea was worth a free Wednesday night meal.

One of the highlights of the church year was church camp. From fourth graders to high school seniors, a huge majority of the church membership headed to Montgomery Bell State Park for a week in the woods.

I was lucky enough to be able to go to camp before I was old enough to be a camper. Mom volunteered to be a counselor and was assigned to a cabin of sixth grade girls.

I became like a mascot to the girls in Mom's cabin. Wherever they went, I went too. The strangest situation was during clothes changing times. I was instructed by Mom to get into my sleeping bag, no peeking. It may have been the hardest assignment I've ever had to complete.

Once I was old enough to be a real camper, I was counting down the days to the start of camp. We boarded the unairconditioned Bluebird church bus, piled high with suitcases and sleeping bags, and headed off to Montgomery Bell.

The camp consisted of the same setup every year. The grounds were very worn, with little grass to be found. Tall trees provided almost complete shade over the entire campgrounds. The boys were housed on the far side of the grounds, in cabins that housed five campers and one counselor each. To reach the boy cabins you had to travel down a steep ravine and back up the other side.

The first task upon arrival at camp was to unload your stuff into your assigned cabin and pick your bunk for the week. I always tried to choose a corner bunk where windows surrounded the side as well as the head.

The next thing on the agenda was a camp meeting in the mess hall. This is where the schedule for the week was revealed, rules and consequences discussed, and the complete camp roster handed out, including cabin assignments.

The cabin assignments were considered as valuable as a gold mine. Knowing where the good looking girls would be staying made it easier to flirt. Of course, elementary boys get more enjoyment out of talking the game than playing in it.

After that initial meeting, we had some free time on our hands. We lined-up at the camp canteen to buy a cache of goodies for the week. Then it was time to stroll around the camp grounds visiting. Occasionally a counselor or another adult would get us to lend a hand in some task, but then it was back to the dawdling.

The dinner bell would ring and that would send us all to the dinner hall for supper. The kitchen crew consisted of church members who volunteered their week to help out at camp. The food was fabulous and meal time was looked forward to three times a day. During meals, we sat with our cabin at a prearranged table. Eating was usually filled with lots of chatter and getting to know new friends and catch up with old ones.

I always wanted a seat at the end of the table near the center of the dinning room. The reason was that at the conclusion of dinner, several things would occur. The first would be a lesson from our pastor Brother Abbington. His minisermons were always directed to children and youth and I remember listening intently to what he was saying. He was able to hold the attention of a room full of young people and get important messages across.

Intertwined with his message would be lots of singing. Glen Cummings was our Minister of Youth and Music and was a blast. Not only was he a talented musician, he knew how to reach young people. I remember singing "Father Abraham, had Many Sons" and "Children of the Lord" (*the Lord said to Noah, there's going to be a floody, floody*) at least once a night. We marched and did the movements and had a great time.

Bro. Glen did a magic trick one night that incorporated a flag and a banana. He told a long story that involved both props. After telling a portion of the story, he would pull down part of the peeling of the banana. I'm not sure how he did it, but at the conclusion of the story the flag was inside the banana. We were amazed, stood and cheered, and begged for him to do it again or at least show us the secret. It became a yearly tradition at camp.

Shortly after the completion of supper, we gathered our flashlights and headed down to the campfire. To get to the campfire we followed a narrow, descending path, riddled with exposed roots ready to send you sprawling. If you were unfortunate enough to have forgotten your flashlight or your batteries died, you were in for a slow, hazardous hike.

When we arrived at the campfire, counselors had already ignited the fire and the blaze lit the entire area. The area bordered the river and had been cleared of all trees and shrubbery. About half way up the clearing was a concrete retaining wall.

We were allowed to sit wherever we wanted and spread out over the entire space. We sang songs, shared personal stories, and listened to counselors and older campers share their testimonies. The campfire time concluded with a devotional time led by one of the church staff.

At the conclusion of one night's campfire, we heard another group somewhere down the river. Bro. Glen counted "one, two, three" and we all yelled "hello" or something to that affect. We waited patiently for a reply and were excited when a reply came back.

We traded messages back and forth a few more times that night and then headed back up the winding path. It was fun to continue this back and forth with the other unknown campers the remainder of the week.

After campfire time, the remainder of the night was free time until the light's out signal was given. There was no doubt where I was heading, the nightly game of spoons.

Spoons is a card game that was extremely fun and somewhat addictive. The minimum number of players is three with a doable maximum of about ten. Each player was dealt four cards and had to keep that number of cards in their hand throughout the game. Placed in the middle of the table were spoons. There would always be one less spoon than the number of players. The goal of the game was to get four cards of the same number or face, i.e. kings or fours.

The game began with the dealer taking one card at a time off the deck of the remaining cards, looking at it and deciding to keep it and discard another card or pass the card along.

This continued around the table as all the players looked for four of a kind. The second part of the game involved the spoons. The first person to get four of a kind would grab a spoon.

There were drastically different ways to go about grabbing a spoon. There were players who were so excited about getting their four like cards they quickly and loudly grabbed their spoon. Others grabbed a spoon as quietly as possible and continued playing the game.

This is where the fun began. Players become so involved in passing cards and looking for certain numbers, it is easy not to notice a spoon being taken. I have been involved in rounds where all spoons were claimed and the game continued because the lone player without a spoon didn't realize all the spoons were gone. Sounds simple but we had a ball.

The additional reason I looked forward to Spoons time was Pam Turley. Pam wasn't a member of our church but came to camp with her friend Angie. Pam was beautiful and I looked for any reason just to be close to her.

The remaining time during the camp days was filled with Bible study, recreational activities like hiking and swimming, crafts, and mandatory down time, or rest.

During one day's free time, a large group of campers were throwing horse shoes. The games were intense as Richie, the camp champ, defeated opponent after opponent. There was a buzz around camp that spread quickly. The news was that Elvis Presley had died.

Church camp only lasted a few more years. The church staff began to change and support for the camp waned. The memories made in the forests and cabins of Montgomery Bell State Park will last a lifetime.

Another summer activity that revolved around the church was VBS, Vacation Bible School. The kids in the neighborhood were part of the VBS circuit. Our parents sent us to every available Bible School.

We went a week at Madison Church of Christ where the JOY Bus came to pick us up. We attended at St. Joseph's Catholic where we made rosaries and listened to the nuns. We attended Rivergate Church of Christ where we chowed down on all the Krystal's we could eat at the week ending celebration. We also attended VBS at our home church, Goodlettsville First Baptist.

I gave my life to Christ at the age of eight. The church was in the middle of revival services.

Carl Duck was preaching and Bill Cox was leading the music and singing many of the solos. On this particular night, Mr. Cox was singing "The King Is Coming". Having been a church goer all my life, I knew exactly what he was singing about and who he was singing to. Jesus was calling to me to accept Him as my personal Lord and Savior.

    We were sitting near the front that night and I quietly slid out of the aisle and met the pastor in the front of the sanctuary. I told him I wanted to ask Jesus into my heart and he led me in a salvation prayer.

    I met with the pastor during the following week and confirmed my decision. I was baptized the following Sunday. The King is coming and He's coming for me.

Chapter 8
Friends of the Family

My parents had many friends as Ray and I were growing up, but probably none more special than the Bryant and Mullinax families. Bobby and Juanita Mullinax had two children, Greg and Kathy. Kathy was the same age as Ray and Greg was three years older than Kathy.

We spent many weekend evenings with the Mullinaxs, both at their house and at ours. Most of the visits centered on our parents playing cards. Our parents played mainly two games. One was Pit, a very fast paced, loud game of swapping cards. You would see each of them repeatedly shouting "two, two, two" and trying to get anybody to swap for the two cards in their hand.

The second card game they played was double solitary, commonly referred to as "Oh, heck" or worse. This game was played much like the solitary made famous on computer systems, only with a partner and against another couple. Both teams played off the same aces sitting in the middle of the table, creating an instant competitive situation. I can still recall the repetitive beat of *swish, swish, smack- swish, swish, smack* as Mom and Juanita furiously ran through their stack of cards as Dad and Bobby manned the more subtle discard pile. When the men were assigned the task of going through the deck the rhythm slowed to a tedious pace.

As our parents played countless hours of cards, we found many ways to entertain ourselves. Most of the time I would find myself with Kathy while Ray and Greg were doing their thing. We played numerous rounds of the board game Life on top of Kathy's bed. Ray and Greg were in Greg's room tinkering with his newest gadget.

One early summer evening while visiting the Mullinax's, Bobby got out their minibike. I had never been on one but wanted to give it a try. The older kids took turns riding up and down the yard as I took in the sights, trying to convince myself to give it a try.

When it came time for my turn, I mustered up the courage and cautiously jumped aboard and headed off. They had a large yard that was completely uphill from the street to the house. Their driveway wound up the front yard, making a long, skinny S before ending to the right side of the house. I headed around the back of the house very guardedly, trying to learn exactly how the bike operated. I took off down the front yard, made a U-turn and headed back up the driveway. Everything was going smoothly as my confidence soared. As I approached the house everyone was signaling that it was time to get off.

I headed towards the group and had every intention of stopping, IF I ONLY KNEW HOW! I realized only then that I did not know how to stop. Not only did I not know how to use the hand break, I panicked and twisted the accelerator.

I took another trip around the house, this time with much less enjoyment. As I came close to everyone again, they started shouting instructions. Due to the loud motor, I couldn't hear a word of their shouted instructions. I decided to take a chance and ditch that crazy machine by sliding off the back of the bike.

My feet hit the pavement and I found myself running behind this cursed contraption. To up the ante', my hand decided to play one last joke and rev the accelerator again. The minibike popped a wheelie, throwing my hands from the handlebars. I fell to the ground, unhurt, as the minibike quickly slowed and was wrangled by Bobby and Dad. I didn't appreciate the humor as much as everyone else. I was still shaken and not happy about the whole situation. The seat of that possessed minibike would never see my rear end again.

My parents asked the Mullinax's to keep Ray and me while Mom went into the hospital to have surgery. We were told she was having toe surgery, learning much later that is was in fact a hysterectomy. I remember Juanita putting me on the leather couch so if I had an accident, it wouldn't ruin a mattress.

Daddy and Bobby made a deal with a family in our church to cut up fallen trees on their property and use the wood as firewood. The Cooks owned several acres of woodsy land in the north part of Goodlettsville. Mr. Marion Cook was a well-respected painter with a specialty in painting barns. His wife, Stella, was a homemaker who spent most of her days caring for their four children.

Daddy would drive our Opel and Bobby would drive his Brat to the Cook's home empty and drive away hours later with a full load of wood. Some days we would make several trips back and forth hauling logs.

I loved to go with Daddy to the Cook's. Occasionally, I would work with the men carrying firewood, but most often I would traipse off into the woods to explore. On the right side of the property was a working barn. There were several animals housed in this barn and I loved to pet those that would cooperate and observe those that wished to be left alone. The loft of the barn begged to be explored and we granted that wish. We climbed up and walked around the loft. We found a rope and decided it would make a good swing. We made trip after trip up the ladder and down by way of a swing ride.

The entire property went uphill from street level, eventually leveling off near the property border at the top of the hill. One day Kathy and I made our way to the top of the hill. It was a snowy day and the ground was covered with two inches of snow. We were enjoying the view from the summit, throwing snowballs, and simply enjoying life.

Out of the blue, a horrible, loud howl came from behind us just past the edge of the Cook's land. We were scared out of our minds and took off down the hill running as fast as our feet would take us. As we jump, rolled, and slid towards the bottom of the hill, we yelled for our dads. Out of breath, scared beyond belief, and still expecting the wolf to come bounding down on top of us, we heard another strange sound.

Coming somewhere from the top of the hill was laughter. Dad and Bobby were making their way down the hill, chuckling all the way. Not until Bobby reared his head back and let out a boisterous howl, did we fully understand. Kathy and I were not sure whether to laugh along with them or do them bodily harm. Bobby would occasionally howl just to goad us about that day.

About halfway up the hill was an old water trough. It was a concrete structure about the size of a refrigerator laid on its side. On a particularly wintry day, with the temperature well below freezing, I found this trough frozen. It contained about three feet of water with the top couple inches frozen.

I found this enticing and jumped up on top of ice. I was having a good time sliding back and forth on top of the trough when the circumstances changed. The ice broke and in less than a second, I was submerged in three feet of nearly frozen water. I jumped out of the water nearly as quickly as I went in. Unsure of what to do, freezing, and scared, I started down the hill to where Daddy was cutting wood.

As I slowly made my way to him, I was finding it hard to walk. My soaked clothes were weighing me down and I was freezing. When Daddy saw me, he hustled me into the Cook's home to Stella.

Mrs. Cook treated me so warmly. She ushered me to the upstairs shower, showed me how to operate it, and left a change of clean clothes for me to change into. I had never experienced such a wonderful shower. The warm water took the chill out of my body.

When I returned downstairs, she had made me a cup of hot chocolate and pushed a chair near the lit fireplace for me to sit. As I snuggled up in front of the fire, I was thankful for people like Stella. As we left the Cook's that day, she returned my clothes to me, washed, dried, and folded.

The Bryant's were the other family our family spent a lot of time with socializing. Grady and Gayle Bryant had two children, Lee who was Ray's age, and Andrea, who was my age. Grady was our family dentist and their family attended the same church we did.

The Bryant's lived on a huge piece of land. Setting at the top of their land was their house, a u-shaped structure that surrounded an in-ground pool. We spent many Saturday afternoons and evenings splashing in their pool along with the Mullinaxs family.

My favorite times at the Bryants were when we swam at night. The lighted pool was a very pretty sight and we usually played some water volleyball or baseball. The diving board provided an outlet for competition; cannonballs, flips, jackknives, swan dives, you name it and we had a contest off the board.

Our three families spent lots of Sunday afternoons at Union Hill Swimming Pool. This huge L-shaped pool had two diving boards (one a high dive), a slide, and two poolside basketball goals. The deep end was twelve feet deep. One unique aspect about the pool was the fact that it bordered a drag strip and you could hear the mighty engines roar when the strip was active.

Most of the Bryant, Mullinax, and Westveer gang at Union Hill Swimming Pool.

The concession stand food tasted great and the jukebox belted out great music nonstop. To this day when I hear certain songs, including the original *Do the Locomotion*, I think of those sunny summer Sundays swimming with friends.

Another family that was involved with our family was the Overtons. The Overtons were our next door neighbors to the right. Bill and Nancy Overton had one son Brian, who was a couple years younger than me.

Daddy worked several evenings a week for the Overtons in their woodshop. They constructed louvers, the triangle apparatus that are found near the roofs of houses that are used for ventilation.

At that time, the woodshop was found in an isolated area in Goodlettsville. Bill Overton, Bobby Mullinax, and Daddy would spend hours repeatedly measuring, cutting, and hammering wood. I loved to go with Daddy while he worked.

Too young to help, my job was to stay out of the way and not injure myself. I explored that entire area from top to bottom. I was on my own adventure as long as I checked in with Dad periodically.

There was a creek that bordered one side of the area. Though I didn't explore that creek in as much depth as I did Dry Creek, it was still a great place to play. Another feature of the woodshop and its surroundings was an outhouse. I had seen pictures of outhouses but had never witnessed one in person. Being the only place to go, that soon changed. This outhouse was an original, not one of those blue prefab kind that dot construction sites today.

It was made of wood, probably the same materials that were being turned into louvers in the woodshop. It had the famous outhouse moon symbol carved into the door and its slats didn't quite touch, creating a breezy toilet time and a view for anyone crazy enough to care.

Another interesting activity centered around sawdust. As the result of hours upon hours of sawing, huge piles of sawdust were scattered throughout the area. Some of the piles were pushing eight feet high. If the pile was fresh, the smell was awesome. The slight burning smell caused by the hot saws combined with the rustic, woodsy smell to create a very memorable aroma.

While the men inside working wore masks to protect their lungs from dust, I climbed those sawdust mountains with the gusto of a Mt. Everest conqueror. I'd go home covered from head to toe in sawdust. It was amazing where the dust would wind-up on your body and how long it could cling to your flesh.

Daddy was a draftsman, drawing churches for the Baptist Sunday School Board in downtown Nashville for more than thirty years. Occasionally I would get to go to work with him. He worked on the tenth floor so the day always started with an elevator ride up to his desk.

He worked at a huge drafting table with a large light clipped to the top. Near the bottom of the desk was a tray that held all of his working instruments. I loved to get hold of his electric eraser. It looked like a small drill and erased very thoroughly and fast. Mechanical pencils, rulers, protractors, compasses, and many other implements filled the space.

Directly in front of Daddy's desk was an extra drawing table. I loved to sit at that table and mimic him. I designed many churches and houses sitting at that table.

While Daddy worked his full day, I found myself doing many things to fill my day. One thing that caught my interest was looking out of the tenth floor window beside Daddy's desk. It seemed as if we were up in the clouds. The people below looked like ants as they walked the streets of Nashville. I spent a lot of time looking at the swimming pool housed on top of a four story hotel across the street. What drew my interest was a fascination with a pool being on top of a building.

I would also visit the Board's library, spending hours looking through the thousands of books, cases of church artifacts, and daily newspapers. Occasionally, I would join the daily tours that showed the inner workings of the BSSB. Daddy had a friend in the print shop who would periodically get me flip pads to doodle on.

The highlight of the day was lunch. We would ride the elevator down to the first floor and head downtown. Along the way Dad would introduce me to everyone who passed as we headed towards Woolworth's, Walgreen's, or many other downtown locations. Even on the downtown sidewalks, Dad seemed to know half the people walking past.

I loved going to work with Daddy, both at the woodshop and the Board. We shared some wonderful times and he inspired me to strive to be my best. While I didn't follow Daddy into the field of architecture, I did pick up on his organizational skills and applied them to my own career.

I would occasionally get to accompany David's daddy, Adrian, to his second job. Adrian's day job was as a site construction manager for the State of Tennessee. His secondary job was as an overnight bowling alley manager.

Adrian was a professional bowling and won several Bowler of the Year awards. In fact, on the day I was born, June 8, 1968, my parents bought a newspaper as a remembrance. On the back page of the sports section was an article about Adrian and his bowling accomplishments.

Periodically, David and I were able to convince Adrian to take us along to Plaza Lanes in the nearby city of Donelson. We were not allowed to bowl at the beginning of the shift. We filled our time playing video games in the mini-arcade, throwing ball or Frisbee in the breezeway just outside the lanes, or watching some of the better bowlers show their skills.

Very late at night, or actually in the early morning hours, we were allowed to hit the lanes. David and I took turns feverously bowling ball after ball until we were signaled that it was time to go. About six in the morning, we would head home, usually stopping for breakfast on the way.

Chapter 9
Fishing

Fishing was a favorite thing for our family to do. We loved to drown a worm and had many favorite places to spend the day fishing. One of my earliest memories of fishing was below the Old Hickory Lake Dam.

We would stop for bait at Trade Winds in Madison and head to our spot. To get to the river you had to carefully scale down a steep, rocky incline. We would head downstream to where the current was a little slower, the embankment somewhat flatter, and a small creek fed into the river.

Daddy would get everybody's lines rigged and hooks baited. When we were very young and just starting to fish, he would even cast our lines for us. It was more like Daddy fishing with three poles and Ray and I figuring out how to make it more difficult for him.

We almost always fished on the bottom when we were at the river. If we were to use a float it would drift downstream and simply make its way back ashore. After our lines were cast we looked for some place to place our rods so we could watch for the tell-tell signs of a bite. Large rocks worked well and sometimes we would simply prop it up on our tackle boxes. Once all the lines were in the water and our poles were propped up, it was time to watch for the end of the pole to bend.

We would stand guard by our poles, looking for any sign of movement. This was problematic because of the nature of river fishing. The river's current dragged the hook and sinker along the bottom. Every time the line would encounter a rock, the pole would bounce.

These bounces would cause Ray and I to grab, over and over again, our rods only to find it was a false alarm. We convinced ourselves that we had just missed catching that whale. If the fishing was slow (meaning we had to wait for more than a minute for a bite) we became bored and look for something else to keep our attention. Skipping rocks across the river was a favorite, but it caused the real fishermen to give us nasty looks, not to mention the danger of finding a snake under a rock.

We did catch some fish in the river, but it did not become one of our regular spots as we grew. I think the danger of rising waters added to our lack of content with the spot. Fishing just below the dam meant we had to stay alert for rising water due to the dam spilling water from Old Hickory Lake. A very loud siren would go off and then the water would start to rise. Never knowing how far the rise would be, we carried ourselves and our supplies way up the embankment to wait and see.

Another spot we fished near the dam was at Rock Island Dock. This was the spot that people put in their boats at the ramp. There were picnic tables, a dock, and lots of shade. The fishing was not good here though the atmosphere was much better than below the dam. We did catch some small ones off the dock and the occasional shad off the shore. We usually got more bites from the geese and ducks than from the fish.

Probably the most productive fishing spot we frequented was near the Dupont Factory. Through the back roads of Rayon city was an inlet just above the same dam we fished below in Hendersonville. The inlet was about 30 feet across and about 150 feet in length from the main part of the lake. We caught lots of brim from this area and the occasional bass or catfish. Trees provided shade most of the time and normally we had the place to ourselves.

We tried many other spots in and around the Goodlettsville, Hendersonville, and Old Hickory areas with varying success. Drakes Creek in Hendersonville would be a hot bed for pan fish at certain times of the year. If the conditions were right we would catch a fish on every cast and not have to wait long for it to happen. Other times we would show up at the same spot and fish for hours with the only bites coming from mosquitoes. Luckily for us, there was a playground directly behind our spot for days the fish were not biting.

We had long been tempted by the creek waters below the walking trail at Moss-Wright Park. There appeared to be sections that could possibly house fish. We finally gave into temptation and gave it a shot.

The first attempt was at the tenth mile marker. Down a steep hill, just off the walking trail was the creek. At this part of the creek, it split into two streams, creating an island in the middle. We crossed over to the island by leaping over the narrowest part of the creek from the bank.

Once on the island, we went to the upstream side and prepared our lines. We had very little success here, landing only the occasional small brim. The fishing was fun and due to spotting a bass passing through we would try again now and then.

The second spot we tried off the Moss-Wright trail was at the four tenth mark. This was a much more secluded area. We made our way down a well-disguised trail to the creek. This part of the creek was slow moving and about twelve feet across. It didn't look like a spot where we would have much success, but we couldn't have been more wrong.

About halfway across the creek was a drop-off, distinguishable only by the darkening of the water. We threw our bait into that pool and, BAM, BAM, BAM, the fish bit fast and furious. We pulled about sixty brim out of that little hole that day. This undoubtedly became our favorite new fishing hole.

The third stop on the Moss-Wright fishing circuit was almost unreachable. Near the seven tenth of a mile marker, we noticed huge fish in the creek's water. It was inconceivable to us that there were fish that big at all, much less in a creek. They were about two feet long and probably weigh fifteen to twenty pounds.

The only problem, though a huge one, was that at this part of the park, the creek was a good fifteen feet below the path and a barbed-wire fence separated us and the fish. We were determined to catch one of these monsters or go down hard attempting.

We carried our poles and equipment down to the spot and made our plan. Luckily it was late fall and the trees were without their leaves. This gave us a better shot at reaching our intended targets. After many tangled lines, lost hooks, and close calls, we landed a few cast near those giants.

It was as if they knew who we were and our intentions. Our attempts to lure them to our baits were totally ignored. Even if our cast landed inches from their giant mouths, these fellows knew better. When you stop to think about it, these Carp didn't get that large by biting every hook thrown their way. In a way, it might have been for the best. I'm one-hundred percent sure had we hooked a fish, we would have never been able to land it.

With Grandma and Grandpa King living in Kingston, Tennessee, a city almost completely surrounded by water, it stands to reason that we did a lot of fishing on our visits. Grandpa was an avid fisherman in his younger days and loved to talk to us about the sport. His love of fishing inspired Ray and me to learn to love it also.

Kingston City Park was about a half mile from my grandparent's house. This park was located on the banks of the Clinch River and offered at least three spots to fish. My personal favorite was the dock that served as the boat ramp. This dock was made of wooden slabs nailed together and held up by sunken telephone poles. The sides of the dock had rubber tires attached to help boats from sustaining damage when docking.

This dock ran about twenty feet into the river and usually had water up to its slats. Occasionally, when the water level was down during drought conditions, the dock's end didn't even reach the water. We would walk from Grandma and Grandpa's house to the park and head straight towards the dock.

The first few casts were always off the end of the pier and thrown as far as possible towards the center of the river. After the initial excitement wore off, we would get about the business of catching fish. It was rare that fish were not biting off the dock, but the best place to cast seemed to change.

Sometimes it was straight down, drawing the fish from under the dock. Other times it was best to cast towards the shore to the right of the dock. And occasionally, we would find success in casting towards the retaining wall near the launching ramp. Just being out on the dock made us feel like we were in our own little boat.

    When we wanted a change of scenery, or the fish just weren't biting, we would take our rod and reels and head towards the park playground. The playground consisted of some swings, a merry-go-round, some rocking horses, and a dome shaped climbing apparatus. It provided a fun alternative for breaks from fishing.

    The second spot we frequented at the city park was the playground's shores. All around the water's edge in this area was flat, grassy land, a perfect place for kids to fish. We would fish our way around the perimeter of the shoreline, walking on the retaining wall while casting. This area wasn't very productive but allowed us room to spread out and walk around.

    The final area that we fished near the city park was below the rocky embankment that was built to keep the main road from eroding into the river. This was the site of the Buffalo Round-Up. Daddy, Ray, and I were not having much luck and were discussing either calling it a day or switching locations.

    When Daddy started to reel in his line, it wouldn't budge. I remember him making the statement that his line was hung up on the bottom. This was commonplace in this area with many rocks on the river's bottom. After attempting to get his line free a few minutes, he muttered something about it possibly being a fish. Back and forth he went; hung, fish, bottom, limb, fish, and so on. I'm not sure how long it took until he was convinced, but there was something alive on the end of his line.

 Daddy fought that giant for about thirty minutes, with Ray and me shouting encouragement and directions the entire time. About fifteen feet off the bank, the creature surfaced. The white belly of a fish shone bright as it rolled in an attempt to free himself.

 Daddy was able to land the giant buffalo weighing nearly fifty pounds. We found an old abandoned trash can and hauled the mammoth fish to our car trunk. We drove back to the King's to show the trophy. Grandpa couldn't believe how big the fish was and said it might be a record. We never looked into whether or not it was a record, but it is still the largest freshwater fish I've seen caught, by far.

 Uncle Earl and Aunt Louise lived in Kingston, too. From their house, we frequented two spots, both providing us with tons of fun. Just across from their driveway were two gravel roads. Each of these roads led to one of our spots. The first led to a spot that produced some big bream. This area was just around the bend from the park, probably a good mile by water, three by car. It was located near a hill that had produced many Civil War relics to treasure hunters.

    To fish in this area, you had to control your cast or chance spending valuable time rerigging your line. Two large weeping willows hung from the bank, creating a leafed dome over the water and shore. The bank was about eight feet above the water, with red clay cliffs making an appearance between the two.

    You had to cast at least twelve feet out to have a chance at catching something. Once your line was thrown and your float was standing at attention, it was time to settle in and wait. We sat on the edge, dangling our feet, waiting for that bobber to disappear. Good fishing, beautiful surroundings, and great company; not a bad way to spend a day.

    The other path leading from the Butler house was to a place we called "The Base". Down that seldom traveled road was someone's dock located on an inlet of the Clinch River. The dock consisted of a plank walkway that led to a metal boathouse, which was capable of housing two boats. The dock ran along the backside of the boathouse and one side.

    The dock was about ten feet long running from bank to boathouse. It was in that small area of water between the boathouse, the bank, and the dock where we fished. We caught tremendous numbers of fish by dropping our lines straight down, though their size was nothing to write home about.

During one day's outing, I remember seeing the strangest looking fish swimming near our fishing spot. It was nearly three feet long and very thin. It had a long pointed nose of about nine inches that looked like a dowel rod. Daddy said it was a Pipe Gar and that he had nice sharp teeth. We decided it would be best to let him cruise on past.

We never saw the owner of this dock in all the times we fished there. One day we found the door to the boathouse ajar and decided to take a peek. The inside of the structure was aglow with a greenish tint. This occurred because the sun was shining through the green tinted fiberglass roof and sides. The eerie coloring combined with the nervousness of being somewhere without permission made us very uneasy.

That uneasiness subsided when we saw the water in the boat bay. The conditions of the lighting allowed us to see deep below the water's surface, and what we saw made our jaws drop. We must have been fishing in the nursery on the other side of the wall while this was where the adults hung out.

These fish looked huge swimming in the water. We scampered to where our poles where and returned to give it a shot. Much like the giant carp in Mansker's Creek at Moss-Wright Park, these guys didn't grow big by pure luck. Fishing was extremely slow and we soon returned to our familiar location on the other side of the wall.

As Ray and I grew, our fishing options expanded. Not only did Daddy get to actually fish when we went fishing, we ventured into the world of casting and artificial lures. We frequented two places in Kingston to try our luck with repeatedly casting lures.

The first was just off of I-40, the opposite direction from Grandma and Grandpa's house. This place consisted of a cove that jutted off from a larger inlet. Grandpa told us that the Strippers, or Stripped Bass, were schooling and should be easy pickins'. He instructed us to buy some lures called Gayblades. Gayblades were about an inch and a half long and very thin. They came in dozens of colors; all trying to replicate a type of bait fish. Each lure had two treble hooks, which were a cluster of three hooks, much like an anchor symbol. On the very tip of the nose of the lure was an eyelet. This is where you tied your line.

We purchased some Gayblades and were ready to put them to work. We headed to the spot that Grandpa suggested and piled out of our Monte Carlo. Little did we know we were about to be introduced to the fast and furious world of Stripe fishing. While Dad and I were still fumbling with our gear in the trunk, Ray made it to the water and hooked a fish on his first cast. That was just the beginning of an unbelievable day of fishing. It was uncommon not to hook a Stripe on every cast. Between us, we would often have three on our lines at once. And occasionally, somebody would land two fish on one cast, one on each treble hook.

The other spot we loved to fish for stripe was at the steam plant. The steam plant was a local landmark with is towering smoke stacks that could be seen for miles around. Our family developed a competition to see who could spot the smoke stacks first on each trip east. The plant discharged lots of hot water into Clinch River, which the fish apparently loved.

We made our way to a point that reached towards the middle of the river. Here we periodically came across the same unbelievable fishing conditions when the Stripe were running. They were easy to spot as they swirled around just under the surface, hunting their next meal. We simply threw our Gayblades into the swarm and wondered. Not whether we would catch a fish, but how big. Most Stripe we caught were about a foot long and weighed a pound or two.

Right below the steam plant was a discharge area. The plant would take in water, mix it with their steam discharge, and release it back into the river. The release point was a man made canal with boulders building up both embankments. The water looked like rapids and the undertow was said to be extremely dangerous. You could fish from the banks or the crosswalk that was built across the discharge point. We didn't have much luck and the danger of the area usually kept us away.

Our family traveled to Fairfield Glade for vacation several times. Fairfield Glade was a startup resort area that was looking for families to invest in property. In exchange for a free stay, my parents would listen to a spill about why they should invest in the resort. Apparently they thought we were good prospects because we kept being invited back.

Fishing was always part of our Fairfield Glade experience. On one trip, Daddy rented a boat and we set off for a day on the lake. We were catching some great fish and had decided to keep the haul for dinner. Late in the afternoon I caught a keeper and pulled up the stringer to add to our catch.

We had a metal stringer that had individual hooks for each fish. As I struggled to put enough pressure on the pin, I lost my grip on the stringer and it quickly disappeared below the water. I instantly became the goat and the topic of many memory sessions as Ray and Daddy retold the story. I held out hope that the fish would swim to the surface and we could retrieve the stringer and save me from the onslaught. No such luck, the fish, the stringer, and our fishing fun for that day were over.

Fairfield Glade provided us lots of other fun, too. Ray and I putt-putted while Mom and Dad listen to the sales pitch. We also watched the residents square dance, caught June bugs and tied strings to their legs to take them for a spin, and rode our bikes.

The only other time I remember fishing with the family from a boat was at Marrowbone Lake, a private lake north of Nashville. We rented a metal, flat-bottomed boat and paddled our way around the lake. Fishing was slow and only endured due to fishing from a boat.

The story that comes from Marrowbone Lake has nothing to do with a fish. We were fishing really close to the shore when Ray got his line hung up in a tree. As he worked to release it, he started hooting and hollering. Still today, he claims he saw a small alligator in the water. As Dad and I failed to buy the story, he became upset. No it wasn't a log, or a gar, or a reflection he claimed. Whatever it was made an impression on Ray and luckily started to share some of the story time with my lost stringer at Fairfield.

Ron Filson and his wife were members of our church and owners of a very successful business. They had a huge piece of property in Goodlettsville and quite a nice setup.
Next to their house was an even more impressive recreation house (the size of many local residences). Also on the property were a tennis court and a swimming pool. All of those amenities were nice, but not the main attraction as far as we were concerned. There were two well-stocked ponds to be fished.

These ponds were rectangle in shape and separated by about twenty feet of land. We mainly fished the upper pond that was closest to the house. This pond was about seventy yards long and thirty yards across. Two docks jutted out into the water on the upper side of the pond. Both docks were covered and had handrails around the compete perimeter of the structure. Located on each dock was a trashcan full of food to feed the fish.

    Our favorite spot was under a weeping willow tree in a corner of the pond. We would throw our lines into the water and wait for our float to go under. It seldom took longer than fifteen seconds for the float to disappear and you knew instantly whether you had hooked a fish or not. The brim we caught at the Filson's pond were not your average pan fish. Many of the fish pushed a pound, which is gigantic for this type of fish. You had a fight every time to land those monsters, and you could catch them all day long.

    We would move around the pond and try different spots, but not for the normal reasons. More so than trying to find where the fish were bitIng, we moved for a change of scenery, to get away from each other, or just to rest. Pulling in lunker after lunker was tiring.

    The lower pond on the Filson property was about the same width as the upper pond but approximately twice as long. The fishing was much slower but the promise of a trophy bass loomed large. This is where the big boys played, where size did matter and quality over quantity played out. I never had much luck on the lower pond and quickly returned to the awaiting sure thing.

Chapter 10
Relatives

I was fortunate to grow up in a very loving extended family that included a wide range of characters. Mom was one of seven children born to Paul and Susie King. Counting spouses, that gave me twelve unique uncles and aunts on the King side of the family.

Uncle Charlie was always my favorite. He was a gentle giant, with a constant chew of tobacco in his mouth. He loved to joke with the nieces and nephews and kept the fun coming. He was a football coach, first at Madison High School in Madison, Tennessee and then at Carson-Newman College in East Tennessee. Uncle Charlie would team up with Uncle Paulie and give me a work over. They would hold me down on Grandma and Grandpa King's living room floor and check my oil, tickle me until I couldn't breathe or wet myself, and check my gut by whopping me repeatedly on the belly. Man was I glad when those check-ups ended. I could tell by the look in the eyes of my twenty-some-odd cousins they were glad it was me and not them.

Uncle Charlie was the one who always made the funny faces in pictures. He would cross his eyes, stick his tongue out, or show us his dentures. I loved to visit his house in Jefferson City and just hang out. Uncle Charlie was a masterful carver and could turn a block of wood into really neat things. For years one of his carvings lit up my bedroom. He made a lamp with a football player's head, complete with a facemask. It was really neat and I was proud to have possession of it. Uncle Charlie never hid his feelings, but I remember watching him cry at Grandma's funeral and thinking what a great man he was and how lucky I was he was my uncle.

Aunt Louise was as crazy and fun as Uncle Charlie. Mom, Ray, and I would jump into the car with Aunt Louise and hold on for an adventure. We would drive through Kingston at breakneck speed having a ball. We would stop at the drugstore for a vanilla coke, run through Handy Burger for a snack, and then just enjoy each other's company. I remember one night in particular that we were all laughing so hard, we pulled over to collect ourselves.

Grandma King was the sweetest person I've ever been fortunate enough to know. I just loved to be in her presence and enjoy feeling her love. She was the ultimate Grandmother. She was heavy set, kept her hair up in a bun, and loved to brag on her grandkids. I loved nothing better than to sit in front of her recliner and wait for her to play with my hair.

She would twist my hair in circles for hours. Her hands were always so warm and soft and I would drift off to sleep. Grandma was a very talented knitter. She would produce afghan after afghan for all the family members. Once I mentioned to her that I would love an orange and white afghan. The next time we visited, she had made me that afghan and also a white and orange pillow cover.

Probably the most embarrassing moment of my childhood occurred at the King's. After playing outside most of the day with my cousins, I came in to go to the restroom. While I was in the restroom I noticed I had a visitor. A tic had attached itself to me and chose a very embarrassing location. Just telling my Mom was hard enough, but I knew better than to just grab and yank the tic.

I told Mom and she tried to remove it without luck. To my embarrassment she went to get help. Grandma and my Aunts Carolyn and Louise returned. Get the picture. Here I am with my pants around my ankles, an uninvited bug stuck to my privates, and four grown women deciding how to remove it. Unfortunately for me, I got the Sampson of tics. The usual methods failed to work and I was ready to call it a pet and let it be. However the episode continued with all the relatives coming to take a peek at the bathroom commotion, each making their own observations and suggestions. The little fella finally let loose, probably out of pity for my situation.

Grandma and Grandpa King's house was a really neat place. It set on one of the main roads through Kingston in East Tennessee. The driveway was lined with a concrete curb that made its way from the main road, down the side of the house, where it divided into three separate parking spaces in the back yard. The front yard was separated from the road with a two-foot high hedge. Fences ran down both sides of the yard separating the neighbors' yards from theirs. The back yard was huge and full of things to do. It was actually divided into three sections: the first was the parking spaces, the second a small piece of grass under a huge tree where Grandpa did a lot of widdling, and the third was the largest portion, which consisted of a lot of trees and a large garden.

The large section of the back yard was fenced in, actually creating two back yards. To go into the large section you would go through a gate and arched seating area. Just through the gate were benches on either side. They were made of white wicker and had vines growing up both sides. It was a really neat place to spend time alone or with relatives. A grapevine grew on the fence down the right side of the yard. It was fun to watch the grapes grow and multiple.

Though their home looked like a one-story house from the front, it was two stories. The yard and drive way sloped down and created a basement type level of the house. From the backyard, about twelve steps lead up to the main living level. These steps were covered with artificial turf and were the location of a great game. "Guess Which Hand" was played by two or more players, usually a group of cousins. One person would be the leader and find a small rock or other item that could easily be concealed in your hand. The rest of the players would sit on the bottom step. The leader would put his hands behind his back and hide the item in one hand. Then both hands would be shown to the stair sitters. Each player would guess which hand the item was hidden in. Those who correctly guessed would move up one step why the others would remain where they were. This continued until someone made it to the top step. That person would then become the leader.

    The bottom floor of the house was never developed into livable space, but was especially good for exploring, hiding from mad parents, or trying to get a break from having to eat ALL the time. There was a door at the base of the steps that led into the bottom floor. As soon as you entered, there was a bathroom on the right. This was the smallest bathroom I had ever been in. You had to pull a string to turn the light on and when you did, creatures scurried away in mass. The most prominent inhabitant was the Granddaddy Long Legs. These guys seemed to be in every nook and cranny of the basement, including the restroom.

From the bathroom there were two small rooms used to store old furniture and miscellaneous items. Then a left turn put you in a sitting type room, complete with a fireplace. This would have made a wonderful "get-away" place had it been finished. Continuing to the left was another room, filled to the rim with old books and magazines. I spent hours in this room looking at the old Reader Digests, especially enjoying the edition from the month I was born. There were a couple old chairs in the room that made it a young boy's dream library. Finishing out the bottom floor was a one car garage, long filled too full of tools to park a vehicle. Grandpa King could have opened up a tool museum with the items located in this place.

Upstairs was where the action was and where we spent most of our time. The main gathering area was the kitchen and the dinning room. The kitchen was always full of the ladies preparing either a meal or snacks. It seemed food was the preferred way to express love. From the kitchen, through the dinning room, was the living room. This is where you would normally find Grandma and Grandpa, relaxing in their chairs. Besides their two recliners, there were also two couches. An old television stood proud on the opposite end of the room. Next to the television was a miniature organ.

I loved to play that organ and drove many relatives from the room by playing, or attempting to play, my favorite hymns from the hymnbook.

My lack of musical talent showed up very young. Competing with the organ in the sound making department was the Grandfather clock located by the front door. The clock chimed every quarter hour and gonged out the appropriate number of gongs every hour.

A large front porch connected to the front door and was normally full of people. The men would go outside to widdle or chew tobacco, or just to get away from the women for a while. It was fun to be in the midst of all my relatives, to hear the stories of fighting in wars, playing college football, and especially about Mom.

Uncle Eugene died of a heart attack prematurely. Totally unexpected, the family wasn't ready for the loss. The relatives came together at the funeral home to mourn his death. Ray and I were much too young to totally understand what was occurring, though I think we did grasp the idea that Uncle Eugene was no longer alive and wasn't going to come back. More out of curiosity than respect, Ray and I were at the coffin looking at the body. It was hot that day and a fan was blowing near the casket.

As we looked at the body, something caught our eye. Uncle Eugene's eyelid moved. Ray and I started screaming and ran for Mom and Dad. Seeking to stop the humiliation that we were causing them, we were rushed outside and given a chance to explain what had happened. We were told that it was impossible and to prove the point, we were marched right back up to the casket.

    Now, a young boy who had just seen a dead person move wasn't too keen on returning to the scene of the experience. However, not being nearly as strong as my parents, I was ushered there against my will. When we arrived, we were assured that Uncle Eugene was still there and no part of his body was moving. However, that statement was proved wrong. The fan that was near the casket was causing his eye lashes to flutter. We had seen movement and were able to prove it. I'm sure Uncle Eugene appreciated the laughter we caused at such a solemn time.

    Uncle David's daughter, Kimmie, came to live with us for a while when I was young. While Mom went to shop at Castner-Knott in Rivergate Mall, Cousin Kimmie took Ray and me to the movies to see the show *Humps*. We were enjoying the movie and the buttered popcorn, very much feeling all grown up. In the middle of the movie, a popcorn kernel attached itself to the back of my throat. It was bothersome and iritated my throat, but wasn't causing any real problems. I tried and tried to swallow and wash it down. That didn't work. I tried to cough and loosen the kernel up. That failed, too. Finally, I leaned over to Kimmie, who was several years older than me, and asked, "Can you choke to death on popcorn?"

    She whispered back, "Yes", unprepared for what followed. I immediately started to scream and wanted my mamma. Kimmie wasn't sure what to do and tried to calm me down. I was having none of that and wanted Momma to save me. She quickly surmised that I was not going to calm down and we set out to find Mom. Ray couldn't believe he had to leave the movie for his hysterical little brother. Mom had dropped us off at the movies and the plan was for her to come back and pick us up when the movie finished. So, without transportation, we hiked over to the mall and found our way to Castner-Knott's customer service. I still recall the PA announcement; "If there is a Joanne Westveer in the store, please come to customer service."

In no time, Momma appeared with a frantic look on her face. Kimmie explained the situation and Mom immediately reassured me I would be fine. (I'm sure she wanted to pinch my head off for scaring her). Mom helped me get the stuck kernel down and things returned to normal. I never did get to see the end of that movie. Ray continues to this day to enjoy reliving the "killer kernel" story anytime he gets a chance.

The majority of Dad's family lived in Utica and Rochester Hills, Michigan. We would occasionally make the long drive up to visit. Grandma and Grandpa Westveer lived in a small house that we crowded into on our visits. Other times we would sleep in the cavernness house of Aunt Norman and Uncle George Caldwell.

Regardless of where we stayed, we had fun exploring these unfamiliar, Northern surroundings. From Uncle Jack's house, we could walk to the corner store and get a Faygo. This type of soft drink was not available in Tennessee at that time. We loved to try all the different flavors including Redpop, Rock and Rye, and many other choices. We would normally have the drink finished by the time we got back to the house. From Aunt Norma's house, we visited a nice little store were we bought pop 'ems, a firecracker type item that popped confetti when you pulled a string.

Grandpa Westveer and Uncle Jack both worked at White Chapel Funeral Home and Cemetery. When Uncle George passed away, we were inside the chapel waiting while Daddy helped his sister, Aunt Norma, finalize the arrangements. We walked around the mausoleum looking at all the dates and sayings on the vaults, at the different art that was displayed around the walls, and explored all the hallways, just trying to pass time.

We found a large box in the corner of the hallway and were curious as to what it contained. We tried to pick it up but it was very heavy. It felt like sand shifting in the box. Daddy and the others came out of the office. We asked what was in the box and were shocked at the answer. Apparently we were right outside the crematorium and had been disturbing someone's remains. We were actually shifting someone's ashes inside the box. How creepy is that?

Daddy and I made a trip to Michigan one year that I'll never forget. We stayed at Grandma Westveer's house and I slept in the front room on a pull-out sofa bed, right next to Grandma's room. Grandma had been having some intestinal problems that were causing her great pain. On the advice of her doctor, she was told not to hold any gas in, but to let it all out. Apparently, she was great at following the doctor's orders.

I'm a pretty heavy sleeper, but I wasn't doing much sleeping during that stay. I have never in my life heard such noises coming from a human being. I think she must have been storing up for years, and when she was given the go ahead by the doctor, she let 'er rip. A thunderstorm would have been less disturbing and smelled far better.

Michigan was not a very safe place for me to be. I endured two fairly serious injuries on trips up north. Our grandparent's had a fruit tree in their back yard. Ray and I decided we wanted to have a snack and what better than fresh fruit. We found a hoe in the detached garage and went to knocking down the fruit. Ray took a big swing and missed the tree completely. The momentum of the swing carried Ray and the hoe all the way around and into my lip. The hoe's blade cut through my lip and the blood started pouring.

I ran into the house and was quickly escorted to the restroom by Mom. We cleaned up my bloody face and eventually got the blood to stop streaming. The question became whether I needed stitches or not. We stared into the mirror and looked at the gaping gash in my lower lip. It had quit bleeding and wasn't hurting too much, so I tried to convinced my parents that stitches were not necessary, knowing fully well that wasn't the case. The decision was made that a trip to the hospital was a necessity.

    We headed to a nearby hospital and I found myself in the emergency room. Luckily, even though my lip ached, it wasn't unbearable and it had stopped bleeding. We were called from the waiting room and I was placed on a bed. The emergency room doctor came and inspected my injury and quickly decided that stitches were indeed needed. A weighted blanket with a small hole in the middle was draped over my entire body. The hole was put over my lips and the doctor began. The shots to deaden the pain hurt worse than the injury itself. Once the area was deadened, it was weird to feel the hook and thread being pulled through my lip. The procedure was quickly over and I and my fat lip returned to the scene of the crime.

    The second injury occurred at Aunt Norma's house. Aunt Norma had a very large front porch that was about ten feet wide from the front door to the first step and it ran the entire width of the front of the house. The porch was a gathering place for the family and the cousins loved to play on and around the porch. One day Norman, Aunt Norma's youngest, and I were running around the porch jumping off of one end and then scampering back up the steps. We were doing lap after lap of our dare devil leaps.

I jumped off the porch and landed on the ground. Instead of popping up quickly and running back to the steps like we had been doing, I hesitated. Big mistake. Norman jumped off and landed right on top of my arm. Though he wasn't a large guy, my arm broke and we took off on another trip to the emergency room in Michigan

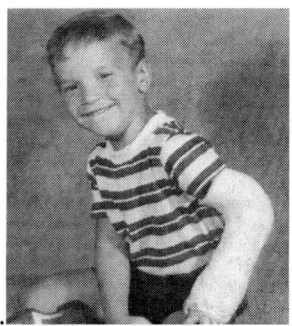

Mike sporting one of his lovely casts!

Ray wasn't the cause of all my childhood injuries, but he was around on a few. While he did swing the hoe in Michigan, he wasn't responsible when I pulled on the cord of the coffee pot and scalded myself as a toddler. Nor did he push me off the top bunk when I was found still asleep on the floor the next morning. However, he was present when I was nearly decapitated by our own swing set.

We had a metal framed swing set that stood in our backyard. It had a slide on one end and three swinging apparatuses in the middle section. One was a type of swinging see-saw, another a regular, run-of-the-mill swing, and the third was a type of carriage swing. It was in the carriage swing that I was hurt (or out of the carriage swing as the case may be).

In this piece of equipment, you sat on a bench facing each other and swung back and forth. Ray and I were swinging in this contraption together, seeing how high we could go and singing the old *Boy and Girl sitting in the tree, K-I-S-S-I-N-G* song. On one particular high swing, I fell out of the seat backwards, or quite possibly was pushed, or maybe even jumped. I tumbled to the ground uninjured. However, the momentum of the swing continued and after reaching its apex on the opposite side, was headed directly for me.

I ducked my head just in time to avoid being hit square in the face; however, the bottom of the carriage hit me in the head, digging into my scalp. It sent me hurtling across the ground, bleeding profusely. The circumstances of what happened next where a blur. The outcome was getting stitches to sew my head back together and an indention in my skull to last a lifetime.

The return visit to the doctor's office wasn't nearly as traumatizing. I remember heading to Dr. Carney's office to get the stitches removed. Dr. Carney came into the examining room and started with the normal friendly chatter. He then took my head into his hands and examined the stitches and seemed to be pleased with what he saw. He turned to leave and I asked if he was going to take the stitches out. His reply stunned me when he said they were already out.

Dr. Carney's office was located in the shopping Mecca of its time, Madison. Located off of Gallatin Road, just past Madison Square and Harvey's, sat possibly the scariest, most reviled place on Earth. His office was the first door in a long, brick structure that ran along side a creek. That foreboding place was as unattractive visually as it was emotionally. The door screeched as you opened it, seemingly trying to warn you to run while you still had a chance.

The waiting room was dark paneled and a perfect square. The receptionist window was on the wall opposite the door, protected by sliding glass windows. After Mom or Dad signed us in, the wait began. It reminded me of being sent to your room to await a spanking. The wait was much worse than the actually punishment. Usually the wait was not more than a day or two, with the trick being to entertain yourself before you went to the slaughter. Every time the door opened to the hallway leading to the patient rooms, I held my breath, pleading that it would be some other victim's name called.

It didn't matter why you had to visit Dr. Carney's office; you were GOING to get a shot, maybe more than one. Knowing this going in was a dreadful thing. In fact, sitting on a table in the middle of all the examination rooms, was a ceramic figurine of a doctor hiding a shot needed behind his back. It should have been Dr. Carney's emblem! Strep throat, shot, sinus infection, shot, stomach bug, shot, check-up, multiple shots, just coming by to say hey, shot, shot, shot. He must have gotten a bonus for every shot he gave to his patients.

Chapter 11
In Closing

During my childhood years, I knew Gateway was a special place, but it took me decades to figure out how special of a place it was to grow up. Gateway was a place where friends, family, and fun combined to make childhood memories and friends that would last for a lifetime. The epicenter for the action was Gateway Elementary School. Not only was the school the physical center of the neighborhood, it was where lifelong friendships were sprouted and dreams began. Having a healthy beginning to life where all adults seemed to be very interested in your success is vital to any youngster, and in Gateway, it was the norm. My parents took a big chance building in this developing neighborhood, not realizing who would be our neighbors and where God would lead, but I am thankful for the risk that they took.

My hope is that all children and families would have a chance to grow up in a special place like Gateway. I have driven through the old neighborhood recently, and I am hoping that a turnaround is coming. Young families appear to be once again taking a risk on their first house and settling in Gateway subdivision.

Thank you for reminiscing with me and taking the time from a busy life to listen to a guy relive his childhood.